Praise for **Outsiders on the Inside** and David Couper.

"His step-by-step guidebook will provide support, tools, and excellent strategies for those 'Outsiders,' empowering them to recognize and own their uniqueness and celebrate the exceptional gifts and talents that they have to offer in a variety of workplaces."
—Drs. Ron and Mary Hulnick, president and Chief Academic Officer, University of Santa Monica

"David teaches the reader to find his/her uniqueness and cultivate it so that they stand out in the marketplace—in a good way. Let David help you find those parts of you that 'don't fit in' and make them special—making you happier in your job and a more valuable worker in your field."
—Martha Elcan, director of Indie feature *Next of Kin* and first assistant director on *Six Feet Under*

"This book is full of excellent insights and helpful suggestions that are enhanced by David's refreshing honesty and his delightful sense of humor. For those who seek support in attaining career success, this exceptional book is an absolute must!"
—M.J. Sawyer, author of *Choosing Sanity* and *That Place Called Sane*

"I've known David for more than 10 years. His ideas are always practical, and sometimes downright transformational. I know several people whose careers were advanced directly because of David's insights and coaching. I've read parts of **Outsiders on the Inside** and can't wait until I read the rest! It's a stroke of genius."
—Shelbra Brinkman, director, Organization Development, Experian

"Knowing the right thing to do in your career is always a tough call and it's even tougher if you don't fit in at work. This book will help all those people who struggle with knowing what to do next."
—Dr. Jeffrey Kahn, liver transplant specialist

"David Couper's work has informed and inspired an intractable rationalist—me—into a career path that seemed utterly beyond my reach. His career advice is simultaneously concrete and inspirational. We attorneys are in the proof business. I can and do attest to the life-changing affect Mr. Couper's advice has had on my career, and thus, on my life."
—Juli Campagna, Visiting Professor of Law, The John Marshall Law School

"What sets David apart from most other coaches, writers, and leaders in this field is an authenticity that comes from profound personal reflection, courageous integrity, and a heart as big as a mountain. And he's smart, too."
—Patric Peake, faculty member, University of Santa Monica

"David holds out the lantern of hope for those who want to be true to themselves while finding career success. I recommend this book to all of my students!"
—Patricia L. Little, PhD, Department of Sociology, California State University

"As a successful outsider myself, I knew the gifts that lay beneath. And now I'm absolutely thrilled to see how David Couper has so clearly liberated this secret into the public eye with his enlightening book, **Outsiders on the Inside**."
—Maddisen K. Krown, MA, international life coach, author, *Huffington Post* Columnist

"David Couper shares the secrets to his own success and that of countless others in turning perceived negatives into positives. Every job seeker will pull invaluable insights and inspiration from reading **Outsiders on the Inside** and applying its principles to their own situation."
—Marilyn Harris, president, Harris/Wolfram Productions, Inc.

"I think we all feel like outsiders at some point in our careers. When you find yourself surrounded by people who aren't in 'your tribe,' this book will give you strategies to leverage your special strengths to create the success you want."
—Donna Schilder, PCC, leadership and career Coach, Glacier Point Solutions, Inc

"Having founded an international recruitment agency and being involved with job seekers for the last 15 years, I know how difficult it can be to find a suitable role for each individual and to find the right person for the right position. This book gives you all the information that you need to effectively position yourself in the market for the perfect job."
—Kate Ferguson, founder and director, People First Recruitment

"'Can I work in corporate culture and still follow my dreams and use my creativity?' That's what the English majors I teach are always asking me. Now David Couper shows how you can make your strengths work for you in the company or on your own account without compromising your true self. Clear, thought-provoking and upbeat, Couper's book opens new possibilities for living a good, fulfilled life, all day long and at the weekends too."
—Dr. Carolyne Larrington, tutor in English, Supernumerary Fellow in English, St. John's College, Oxford University

"I was delighted to read David Couper's pithy and timely guide to career success. His message is as neat as his method is simple and should enable even the squarest peg to fit in the roundest hole."
—Michael Arditti, award-winning novelist

"David's personal experience and professional knowledge is the perfect combination. **Outsiders on the Inside** is a 'must have,' a 'must read,' an invaluable guide to success!
—Suzanne Lyons, independent producer

"David Couper is a trail blazer in the coaching world, and he is just now publicly sharing his secrets about how to have a successful career. His experience, intuition and integrity make this book stand out from the rest."
—Morgana Rae, internationally acclaimed life coach, author, and professional speaker

How to Create a Winning Career...
Even When You Don't Fit In!

Outsiders on
the Inside

David Couper

**CAREER
PRESS**

Pompton Plains, N.J.

Outsiders on the Inside
Edited by Kate Henches
Typeset by Gina Hoogerhyde
Cover design by Faceout Studio Designs
Printed in the U.S.A. by Courier

To order this title, please call toll-free 1-800-CAREER-1 (NJ and Can-ada: 201-848-0310) to order using VISA or MasterCard, or for further information on books from Career Press.

The Career Press, Inc., 3 Tice Road, PO Box 687,
Franklin Lakes, NJ 07417
www.careerpress.com

Library of Congress Cataloging-in-Publication Data
Couper, David, 1960-
   Outsiders on the inside : how to create a winning career--even when you don't fit in! / by David Couper.
       p. cm.
   Includes index.
   ISBN 978-1-60163-127-5 -- ISBN 978-1-60163-722-2 (ebook) 1. Career development. 2. Personality and occupation. I.
Title.
   HF5381.C6935 2010
   650.1'3--dc22

                                                                    2010025467

CONTENTS

INTRODUCTION

My mission in life is to educate and entertain and, this is also my mission for this book!

I intend to educate you about how you can go from being an outsider to an insider without giving up who you are and without having to settle in any way. I want to acknowledge all those people who, like I used to, struggle with work, and who dread Monday and long for Friday, because they feel so out of place and unvalued in their careers. My heart goes out to all those people who feel like they work only to pay the bills and are counting down the time until they can leave. I love to educate people about how it doesn't have to be that way, and to help them find a way out of this work trap to a place where they are happy when beginning a new week.

This book should also entertain. It contains stories of my life, which includes living in Japan, England, and the U.S.A. both in the midwest and on the West Coast, experiences gained working with companies and organizations all over the world in fields from faith-based hospitals to fancy-priced hotels. There are also case studies, examples, and stories from as diverse a group as you could imagine, including Greta Garbo, Ben and Jerry, and Copernicus. From my 20 years of coaching clients I am also lucky enough to have many examples of how outsiders became successful insiders, including those working in manufacturing and movies.

As you read this book, I want you to be able to pick up new job-hunting techniques, be introduced to career change tools, and be given the opportunity to try out new ways of looking for a new job or changing work. Many of the books that claim to tell you how to find a new job just don't work, especially for the person who is struggling with fitting in. I know from my 20 years of coaching and consulting experience, and from my own personal experience of being laid off and having to find a new job, what is effective and what isn't in a job search. I am honored to be able to share some of those secrets so you can be living the work life you dream of.

But why this book, and how did it come about? It all began when I first noticed that in one job, in one country, I was an outsider, who didn't fit in with the culture and didn't work out as an employee; but in the same job, for the same company, in another country, I was still an outsider, yet I was successful at the work and was treated as an insider.

As a result I began to wonder: What made the outsiders who became insiders different? Was it in their genes, or could it be taught? If it could be taught, could I teach it? The answer was yes. Yes, outsiders could be taught how to turn their differences to their advantage and become these successful insiders without giving up their identity. There was a process that made sense and was proven to be successful.

It was very exciting to discover what this process would look like. For more than 10 years I learned about the process through my own and clients' experiences. It then took another five years to put the material together, get it ready as a book, and work through to publication.

On the journey from idea to publication I had to also learn about myself.

In this book you will be introduced to tools and techniques that will help you have a winning career. Instead of getting stuck by feeling like you don't fit in, you will be able to break free by valuing yourself and what you can offer. In a structured, transformational, and informative process you will learn how you can become an outsider on the inside. I hope you enjoy the journey. Let me know how your experience is. I always love to hear feedback. Good luck with your career, and may your dreams come true.

David Couper
www.davidcoupercoach.com

ARE YOU A WORKPLACE OUTSIDER?

My very first job was teaching English in Japan. That was also when I first realized what it means to be a workplace outsider.

It was the early 1980s, and I had been selected to be part of a joint Japanese-British program that sent British graduates like me to Japan, to teach English. At the time, Westerners were fairly rare in Japan and the culture—historically distrustful of foreigners—had not opened up as it has now. I had been dispatched to an engineering company in Yokohama, outside Tokyo, where I was to develop the communication skills of its employees. This was vital, as 80 percent of the company's work was designing and constructing oil refineries in the Middle East and Africa. Although I had taken some Japanese language and culture classes, as part of my orientation, I wasn't prepared to be an outsider.

I was assigned to the engineering company's human resources department—the only white, British, 6-foot-2-inch, non-smoking foreigner. I was different. I stuck out. I was noticed—big time. The word that the Japanese use for foreigner is gai-jin, and that literally means an "outside person."

This is not to say that I was treated badly. In many was I was an honored guest. I was paid handsomely and provided with an apartment, free flights back to England, and a television with programs both in Japanese and English. But people stared at me in my British suits. They talked about me in Japanese right in front of me. And they commented on my skill with chopsticks even though I was not much better than a kindergartner at dealing with slippery tofu, managing a fried egg, or picking up peas.

At first it was fine. I was in the honeymoon phase. Everything was new and interesting—but then it became uncomfortable. I would some-times be refused service in a restaurant, or a hotel would mysteriously be full even though a Japanese-speaking person had made a reservation for me. Or I would not be allowed into a bar because it was for Japanese only.

I read every book I could find about the Japanese culture, and, just as I thought I understood it, something happened that tripped me up. The final straw came after I became sick. I was out of the country on vacation—a negative for my boss, who didn't see why I needed to go to another country nor why I needed to take time off—and I picked up a liver infection. Having something wrong with your liver makes you incredibly tired and debilitated. I was in hospital for three weeks until I was restored to health.

One of my guide books told me that if someone is sick in the hospi-tal, the company will collect money from your coworkers and come to your sick bed to present this gift to help you with expenses. I didn't need the money for my treatment, as I had insurance, but I did expect a visit and a basket of fruit or a bouquet of flowers. Three weeks went by and finally my boss showed up, without any gifts—not even a stick of gum, and certainly no envelope full of cash. His main focus was whether I was going to be well enough to come back to work. He spent more time talking with the doctor about my condition than visiting with me. I left the job soon after that.

I spent another two years in Japan split between the British Council and a company that was the agent for BBC English, and then I went back to the UK and took a course in writing training programs for adults. From there, I ended up working for Arthur Andersen, a major international accounting firm with an office in London. It was then that I realized what it was like to be an outsider, not because I was physically or ethnically different as I had been in Japan, but just because I felt different.

It all became very clear when my boss told me I was wearing a "career-limiting tie." At first I thought he was joking, but I soon realized he was dead serious. His comments weren't just about style. They were about substance—my substance.

On that particular gray London day, I was wearing a tie bearing the American flag, a striped shirt, and a houndstooth suit. Maybe not the smartest of fashion choices, but, still, that was just me. My colleagues all wore the same uniform every day: dark suits, white shirts, and power ties. The women had their own version of this prescribed attire: dark suits and white blouses with large floppy bows. I was a colorful peacock among a flock of gray pigeons, and, visually, I clearly didn't fit in. But my fashion sense was just the tip of the iceberg. Deep inside, I felt I didn't belong. Every conversation I had, every memo I read, and every person I met seemed to scream "outsider" at me. I felt just as much a foreigner with my London employer as I had in Japan.

Apart from looking different, I *was* different. It was 1986 and the heyday of the yuppie. My employer hired the best fresh MBAs, paid them well, and then demanded that these new graduates dedicate their lives to the company 24/7. In return, if you played the game well, you would become rich and powerful. The biggest of big cheeses in the firm had all the trappings of success—a handful of houses, outstanding wine collections, and the best seats at the opera—not that they had time to enjoy them.

I worked to live, rather than lived to work. I wanted balance. I wanted to spend my free time with friends, not clients; write something that would make a difference, not generate a lot of fees; and, most of all, I wanted to retain my soul.

Clearly, I was different from the powers that be. I talked about plays I had seen; my bosses talked about the plays they had made in the market. I discussed how we could help the poor; the firm wanted to help themselves become richer; and I loved to cook Italian, but it sometimes seemed as though the clients only wanted to cook the books.

All this would have been tolerable had I enjoyed my work and felt that it was valued, but I didn't and it was not. I wanted to write. My boss wanted me to edit. I wanted to push the envelope. My boss wanted me to stuff the envelope. I wanted to be funny ha-ha; my boss thought I was funny-weird. I was a workplace outsider and clearly a mismatch for my job.

You've likely heard the expression, "It's like trying to fit a square peg into a round hole." That's how outsiders often think of themselves. But where did the expression originate? Years ago, when carpenters built a house or made a piece of furniture, the wood was joined together with wooden pegs. A round peg fits exactly into a round hole. A square peg—one that hasn't been shaped by a carpenter—won't fit into a round hole. A square peg falls through the hole, is too tight to fit, or has to be forced into the hole. At best there will be a gap around the peg that will let air through. At worst the wood will split. If you are building a house, the pegs may come loose and the house might collapse. With such potentially dire consequences, it's no wonder the notion of trying to fit a "square peg into a round hole" was so powerful.

My first job out of college was at a sporting equipment manufacturer. That kind of place attracts a lot of "jocks" and wannabe "jocks." I came into that environment as the smart kid from a good school, and these people felt it was their right to harass me as much they as they wanted. I really couldn't relate to my coworkers because they were all married with children. Also, for them, it was a just a job, and I was genuinely interested in the technology I was working with. It was a terrible fit.
—Alexandra Levit, author, *They Don't Teach Corporate in College,* Career Press

Aliens and Square Pegs

What are workplace outsiders? They can be nonconformists who are not part of the team. They struggle to be like other employees, to blend in, but fail, and have to work hard not to say the wrong thing or do something embarrassing. Or they can seem as though they run with the pack, but actually inside they are being eaten up with lack of fulfillment and happiness. Or they can be the freelancers and consultants who keep not being asked back to a client to do work because they are too "out there." Or even entrepreneurs who struggle to be like other entrepreneurs and always seem to be off base.

Here's how one of my coaching clients explained it:

> *I've been a sales executive for 20 years in many high-pressure environments. I was good at what I did, I focused on my clients and on my sales, and tried to cope with my bosses, fellow employees, and work environments. In my last job, I could no longer just keep my head down. I didn't fit in with the corporate culture or values. The boss considered the department I was in to be a "loser" department. Clients were viewed as "inventory." Contracts with clients were not based on trust or service, but on extracting the greatest commissions, even after they left the agency. There were a few executive "pet" employees, but in general execs and their assistants were treated dismissively and is if they were replaceable.*
>
> —Pat, former sales executive, consultant, Entertainment Industry, Los Angeles, California

Outsiders, even if they look "right," are, in reality, just afraid of doing something that makes them stand out as nonconformists. Or they may be very good at their jobs, as experts, but they are always waiting for the other shoe to drop—a stiletto that will pierce their self-esteem, a boot that will squash their morale, or a flip-flop that will slap them down for their spirit. Workplace outsiders are always worried about losing their jobs.

One client who was an administrative assistant took no vacation and always worked weekends and stayed late because she was fearful of what would happen at her job. She was scared of getting canned even though everyone loved her work.

The average workplace outsider is usually unfulfilled, unhappy, and desperate for a change. Or even worse, they've given up hope of a better work life. Many feel as if they are aliens working on another planet, their boss is a Martian, and their coworkers speak Klingon. Not only do they not know how to fit in, but they also usually don't know how to be a success or find fulfillment in a workplace where they feel like outsiders.

A talented friend of mine dressed as if she was stuck in a 1960s time warp. People laughed at her behind her back and she couldn't get the breaks she deserved.

Some outsiders may seem to eventually, always, mess up. I think we can all understand the person who makes the jokes at the wrong time, does not get promoted because his ideas are just too wide of the mark, or who is always switching jobs hoping to hit that dream job but ends up quitting before she gets fired.

Nick was like that. At the age of 35, he had never stayed in a job longer than a year. He either got fired or left in a storm because he had such trouble fitting in. He said this about his first job, at a Detroit ad agency servicing an automaker client.

Other outsiders look like superstars. The person who has the great job and seems to be on top of the world may also be an outsider, struggling to find his or her true calling. This type of outsider is very smart, will deliver the goods, yet will still not be happy in his own skin.

One example that sticks in my mind is a good friend, Richard, who worked his way to the top, becoming head of HR for a large company only to confide in private how he hated his job and had always wanted to do something more creative.

Another outsider subset is the person who is exceptional but cannot make her career work. Outsiders may come up with solutions for problems that their company does not want to solve, or they may not want to solve the problems about which the company is passionate.

One of my coworkers spent three weeks developing a corporate message that was fabulous, fun, and focused—unfortunately, it was two weeks too late.

As a trainer and coach for the last 20 years, I've worked with hundreds of people who have struggled with fitting in, and I've learned that outsiders come from varied personal backgrounds and are found at every level of the workplace.

My story begins two decades ago when I first arrived in America, unable to speak English, with hardly any money, and without any friends and family.

After driving a taxi on the streets of Chicago for three years, I worked in several sales jobs, until I came across an opportunity to work for Nextel Communications. Intimidated by the white color environment, my heavy accent and broken English kept me feeling that I did not belong and therefore did not perform as expected. I was afraid to speak to customers, because of the possibility of failure.
—Ron Shimony, speaker and author, Schaumberg, Illinois

You can be a rich outsider or a poor one, female or male, religious or non-believer, gay or straight, a CEO or a busboy. Being an outsider is about not fitting in—plain and simple. Being a successful outsider is about not fitting in and celebrating it—whether it means you find a company that loves your uniqueness or you stay with the same company but find a different department or change the focus of your existing job. Here are just a few examples:

Teri, a brilliant industrial psychologist who has a PhD from a well-known university, dressed like a bag lady and worked in a corporate role. Her ideas might have been stunning but what stunned her boss was how she could look like she just got out of bed. Her whole life was spent defending her attire instead of her scientific theories. She longed for someone to listen to her ideas, respect her knowledge and forget that she wore mismatched pumps three days running. She wanted to get on with her job in peace instead of at war with the fashion police.

Richard gave up his dream of a being a copywriter for an ad agency and became a human resources manager instead. He felt bored, frustrated, and even desperate as he wrote about current and exciting changes in the 401K policy instead of working on the winning tag for the current and exciting changes in the BMW 5 Series. He worked hard for a modest salary where the only excitement was the bi-annual department potluck. Things were so bad that he sometimes felt that pot might be the only way he'd get through another Open Enrollment for the new dental benefits plan.

Hannah spent 20 years working towards senior vice president at a large company, only to discover that she did not have a head for management heights and hated being at the top of the pile. The company politics, the manipulation of power, and the "hiring and firing philosophy" made her sick. She needed happy pills to get her through the day and a bottle of wine to get her through the night. Hannah was counting the years until she could retire and was praying that her body would not give in before her pension paid out. Her team returned the favor by loathing and despising her. She wanted to be on stage, performing and creating instead of selling her soul.

Teri, Richard, and Hannah are outsider square pegs trying to fit themselves into round hole workplace environments. Their work lives were not working and they were desperate to make a change but didn't know how to start.

Later in the book we'll find out how these people were able to accept their outsider uniqueness and turn it into an asset. But first, let's take a closer look at what outsiders have in common.

The Five Outsider Traits

Whether you are an executive or an executive's assistant, a shop owner or a clerk, if you are a workplace outsider you share several of the following Outsider Traits:

1. Outsiders look different.
2. Outsiders sound different.
3. Outsiders act different.
4. Outsiders feel different.
5. Outsiders are made to feel different.

As we explore each of these traits, see if you can identify yourself as a workplace outsider.

1. Outsiders look different.

An outsider's appearance can engender racist, ageist, sexist, homophobic, or simply derogatory responses. Looking differently than your workplace peers is perhaps one of the most common outsider characteristics.

Our ethnicity often makes us feel different. As discussed earlier, I worked in Japan for four years, and for the first time in my life I felt different because of my race. Within the company people were polite and didn't mention my obvious differences to my face, but behind my back they gossiped.

They talked about how tall I was, marveled about my big nose, and even wondered about my hazel eye color. People greeted me by saying takai, which I eventually realized wasn't another way of saying hi but translated as "tall" or "wow, he's a giant." Instead of having my career based on my work product, my bosses focused first on how I looked different. And the ironic thing was that my key job qualification was being foreign.

Your gender can also mean that you look different at work. If you're a male nurse or a female CEO, your mere appearance likely stands out and makes you feel like an alien. It is assumed that men are doctors, not nurses, and women are still under-represented at the higher levels of the corporate world. So in both instances, "looking different" can mean feeling like an outsider. An aggressive female executive might be called a shrew and made to feel like an outsider, even though aggressive male executives are praised for their shrewd leadership qualities. A man who wants to be a nurse will face a stigma in his personal life and at work. He may be accused of lacking drive or settling for second best by old-school relatives who think that he should be a doctor rather than doing "women's work." His coworkers may assume he is the stereotypical gay male nurse. Such biased reactions only add to the outsider's sense of isolation.

Feeling like an outsider because of your appearance goes beyond ethnicity or gender. Research has shown that many hiring decisions are based on how people look. The person who fits a standardized image of the prospective employee is more likely to get the job than someone who looks unusual in any way. Applicants who are overly short or tall, fat or skinny, likely have less chance of getting the job than someone who is considered average or "normal."

Research has shown that the more attractive the candidate, the likelier the chance the person is hired. ("Physical Attractiveness Bias in Hiring: What is Beautiful is Good," Comila Shahani-Denning)

2. Outsiders sound different.

How you sound to others can also cause coworkers and colleagues to treat you like an outsider. If you have a regional or foreign accent, an unusual speaking style, or if you speak softly or loudly, others may brand you as remarkably odd. A woman with whom I worked had a strong foreign accent and was often passed over for opportunities to represent the company at conferences or seminars. She was a well-qualified, articulate expert but never landed those jobs because of her accent.

Peculiar speech patterns can brand one an outsider as well. For example, the popular TV show *Seinfeld* featured an episode about "low-talkers"—people who speak softly. A woman Jerry Seinfeld was dating was ridiculed as an outsider, when her crime was simply not talking loudly enough for Jerry to hear her over the clinking glasses in a New York City restaurant. In telephone sales, where your voice is your main tool there is no room for anyone like Jerry's would-be girlfriend who does not speak loudly and clearly. Low-talkers must learn to speak up, or must find a niche where low-talking is acceptable or, better still, appreciated.

Sadly, outsiders often resort to being silent rather than face ridicule for a particular speech style, accent, or vocal habit. In the training classes I teach, I've found that those who say the least, perhaps because they feel like outsiders because they are not confident, or because English is not their first language and they are embarrassed about their language skills, often have a lot to contribute. They'll come up to me after the class and say how much they enjoyed the training. Their comments reveal a deep understanding of the topic, but because they feel they don't fit in, they don't participate in class discussions and are under appreciated.

3. Outsiders act different.

A range of behaviors can make you stand out in a less than positive way in the eyes of your workplace colleagues. It may be that you prefer to bring your lunch rather than join the dine-out crowd. Or maybe you keep a framed photo on your desk of you and your same-sex partner in a loving embrace. Or perhaps you believe that taking the bus to work is an important choice for the environment when none of your peers ever venture onto public transportation. A friend of mine fits this latter category. Not only did her coworkers look on her as an outsider for not owning a car, but they also resented having to occasionally drive her to meetings outside the office. She was thought of as an environmentally conscious inconvenience—and an outsider.

4. Outsiders feel different.

Even though on the surface you might look and act just like everyone else at work, inside you may feel like a outsider. Your worldview or lifestyle may be different. If you were brought up in another country, or raised in a different tradition, you may feel that you don't fit in culturally. A coaching client who was Jewish felt like the odd woman out when Christian prayers were said at the beginning of business. And some clients feel different for less obvious reasons—they simply sense that they aren't on the same wavelength as their workplace peers.

A friend of mine whose father was a union leader struggled with outsider feelings when he worked for a traditional corporation that focused solely on the bottom line without regard to worker welfare.

I met "Corinne" while working for Arthur Andersen in Chicago. She spoke four languages, had lived in various cities throughout the world, and found herself teaching English to foreign executives in the Chicago head office of a large U.S. corporation. She enjoyed the work and liked interacting with students from all around the world. So she was happy when they hired her on full time. But when she was transferred to a job as an instructional designer, writing training materials, she found she was not using her language skills. But more than the work itself, she also found that the culture was different—she was working in the suburbs with other instructional designers and project managers. Most of her coworkers had never traveled and didn't understand Corinne's references to the European lifestyle. Whenever she talked about Europe, where she grew up, she began to believe that they thought she was showing off. So Corinne refrained from talking about what she loved and instead stuck to more familiar topics—cooking and television. In an attempt to share her knowledge with her coworkers, she brought her favorite Italian dishes to work and bought colleagues tickets to foreign films—but her efforts didn't make her feel any less of an outsider.

Corinne confessed that because she felt so out of step with her colleagues, she found it painful to go to work each day.

5. Outsiders are made to feel different.

Too often, coworkers and bosses draw attention to whatever it is that makes the outsider stand out. A sales executive who is also a talented painter found this out to her dismay. She mentioned to her boss that her work was being exhibited in a local gallery, and rather than congratulate her, he ridiculed her in front of coworkers as "our little wannabe Picasso." After that, instead of being taken seriously as a high-performing sales exec, this talented outsider was treated as an amateur dabbler and a joke.

Bosses may also make you feel like an outsider for being associated with a corporation that is no longer in power. For example, after a corporate merger, a manager may make a point of talking about which employees come from the "winning company" and which don't. In front of others, they might sarcastically ask you, "So, why not enlighten us about how you processed orders with that old company before we took it over?"

Some of us may not even realize we are outsiders until rude or insensitive coworkers or policies make it quite obvious. For example, although freelancers often do exactly the same work employees do, they can be made to feel like unwanted outcasts. Freelance workers have told me that not being invited to lunch with the staffers, or to the company Christmas party, can dampen their morale and negate any sense of being part of the team.

Whatever the reason for being branded as different, when you are defined by one or more of these Outsider Traits, work can become a dreaded ordeal rather than an opportunity to build meaningful connections to people and let your talents shine.

The Negative Impact of Being an Outsider

Whether you have only one or all five of the Outsider Traits, your career and personal life are likely affected in a number of unpleasant ways. Until you learn to make your outsider uniqueness work for you instead of against you, being an outsider is not fun. It depletes your energy and kills your spirit.

At the accounting company in London at which I wore the career-limiting tie, I was never myself from the day I was interviewed for the job to the day I was "counseled out," which was a polite way of saying I was asked to leave. While working at this job, I couldn't reveal who I really was, couldn't do what I did best, and couldn't get respect for my efforts.

I hated my job and didn't know what to do to turn my life around. I became depressed about my lack of success, which inevitably spilled over into my personal life. I dreaded Sundays because I knew Monday was coming. Rather than enjoy my weekends off, I sank into a deep depression. When Monday rolled around I couldn't wait until Friday. During the week, I would escape the office as often as possible, going out for cappuccinos at least four times a day to get away from my desk, taking long lunches, and disappearing into a file room to "find something." I hated every minute of being at work.

Outsider feelings affect your life

Often a work issue or career problem can hurt other parts of your life. When I worked in London in a job with which I was unhappy, I also had issues with finance. I spent far more than I earned to make myself feel better temporarily. I thought I deserved to have nice meals out, live in a fashionable part of town, and be able to go abroad when I wanted to.

It also is no surprise that romance does not fare well with career issues. When I counseled expatriates in Japan, the most common issue sending them home before their assignment ended was their relationship with their spouse. The employee often started out as an outsider in the new foreign environment but could overcome the problems of the job to become a success, whereas the spouse felt like an outsider from the outset and the feelings never changed.

Romantic relationships suffer as do family relationships. Outsiders spend time trying to make other people happy, working long hours, doing work that does not pay well, or covering depression and desperation with drink and drugs.

Years and several careers later, once I began coaching others who suffer as workplace outsiders, I began to see even more clearly how miserable we can become unless and until we address our outsider predicament.

For instance, Hannah, the senior vice president at a large bank (we met earlier), found that all her ideas at work seemed to get shot down, no one respected her point of view, and she always seemed to get the assignments deemed most likely to fail. She had to shout to make herself heard, complain if she wanted to get anything done, and threaten if she didn't get her way. Prior to holding this particular position, Hannah had been a positive person with a great personality, a big heart, and a gentle nature. Now she had become cynical and negative. Instead of being a leader in her organization, she became a naysayer, a person who sees problems in a proposed solution even before the solution is described. Hannah's colleagues avoided her because they believed she was toxic. Her boss didn't support her, she wasn't promoted, and she was given the tasks that other people didn't want. She hated her job and her job hated her. She was counting the years until she could retire—until she realized that work could be so much more fulfilling than that.

With some training, she healed herself, regained her gentle spirit, and rediscovered her love of children. With help from mentors, she developed a childcare program for her company, which she runs. Now she gets to be a child at work and get paid for it. Her gentleness and big heart are essential for her new job.

It's not just high-powered managers and executives who pay the price for being individualists and not fitting in. Susan, a machine operator, was smart, eager to learn, ready to take on more responsibility—yet she didn't fit in. It sounds crazy that someone who's a star performer is also an outsider square peg, but it was because she was a star performer that Susan didn't fit in. Her supervisor, a nice guy but a poor manager, was a control freak. He didn't reward machine operators who thought for themselves. In fact, they were encouraged to "leave their brains at the door."

Susan was different. She took responsibility for her job and would stop the production line if she noticed a problem with quality. One time she noticed a problem with the sealing process; the seals weren't perfect, causing the contents to leak and damage other cans. The entire batch was in jeopardy. Because her boss was out at a meeting, Susan took it upon herself to stop the production line until the mechanics could fix the problem.

Rather than being rewarded for preventing a major quality control calamity, Susan was given a disciplinary warning for stopping production. She was told she should have waited and reported the problem to her boss when he got back. Had she waited, the choice would have been to ship inferior product or dump the whole production run, worth thousands of dollars.

Susan's fellow team members thought she was nuts for causing problems. Her union representative didn't want to fight her battle. The lack of support and the stress caused her to lose sleep and develop a nervous skin condition. She was miserable, but she had to keep working. She had a mortgage, three kids, and an ex-husband who didn't pay child support.

Susan kept her job, but became known for having an attitude problem. She didn't get the promotion she deserved and was heading for a blowup with her boss—and a breakdown.

Once coached to learn about and celebrate her uniqueness, Susan began to value her education, and her ability to understand the big picture and spot problems. She looked around the plant for opportunities where her abilities would be valued. She found it in Quality Control. The QC group needed someone who could relate to the job and the employees, but could also analyze and make decisions about process and systems. She was perfect for the job and she loved the position. She was valued for her expertise, brainpower, and ability to understand the operator's point of view!

Can you relate to what Susan and Hannah went through as the result of not fitting in with their workplace colleagues? Can you relate to the toll it can take on you when you're labeled an outsider at work? Next, you have the opportunity to assess your workplace outsider profile.

Self-Assessment: Are You a Workplace Outsider?

Take this quiz and find out if not knowing how to be unique at work might be holding you back from the career satisfaction you deserve.

Answer YES or NO as honestly as you can:

1. At lunchtime do you usually eat alone?
2. Do you work alone most of the time?
3. Are your ideas usually embraced by your coworkers and your boss?
4. Are you happy to model yourself after your boss?
5. Do you socialize with your colleagues on a regular basis?
6. Do you race to get home at the end of the day?
7. Do you often work late or on weekends?
8. Do you argue a lot with your colleagues, or want to?
9. Do you often receive negative comments about what you wear or how you look?
10. Do you prefer to spend at least five years in one job?
11. Does your boss understand and focus on your priorities?
12. Do you run your own business or work freelance?
13. Do you enjoy working in a large organization?
14. Do you believe strongly in your organization's philosophy?
15. Do you work only for the paycheck?
16. Do you have a lot of fun at work?

Answer Key

Award yourself one point for YES answers to the following questions: 1, 2, 6, 8, 9, 12, 15.

Add your total score. Read the following description to see how much of an outsider—a square peg trying to fit into a round hole—you are in your workplace.

"Round peg"
2 or lower

Most of the time you fit in with your work environment. Occasionally you may feel uncomfortable at work, but usually you feel in sync with your coworkers.

"Round/square peg"
3 to 5

Sometimes you feel that you fit in at work, and other times not. At times you feel uncomfortable among your coworkers because you sense that you're not on the same wavelength.

"Square peg"
6 to 8

Most of the time you feel that you don't fit in at work. You feel alienated from and uncomfortable among your coworkers.

Interpreting your quiz results

If you are a round peg, congratulations. You fit in well with your workplace environment. Fitting in is great, but it can also prevent you from reaching new heights in your career. Standing out, on the other hand, can be a great way to succeed. Throughout this book you'll discover the advantages of standing out in a positive way.

If you are a square peg or a round/square peg, be assured that in the chapters to follow you will learn how to transition from being an unhappy outsider to a satisfied, successful one. Remember too that you are perfect as you are. The objective is not to become more of a round peg, but to make your "square-peggedness" work for you.

Some of you may disagree with your quiz results. There are two possibilities.

First, the results could be inaccurate. Go with your own understanding of yourself, with how you feel. No quiz is infallible. The second possibility is that the results could be correct but you may not want to believe them. If this is the case, you will need to reflect on your response to the quiz results. What are the fears that come up for you? What makes you unable to accept yourself as a square peg?

2

DISSENTERS, ODDBALLS, AND MAVERICKS RULE!

Outsiders are found in all companies and organizations, and many of them, maybe most, are not as successful as they could be. At some point in our lives we realize that we're different. We logically follow the societal norm that values conformity, and that leads us to decide that being different is a bad thing. A natural but huge leap. We decide that we should be like other people. We see pain in being an outsider and pleasure in fitting in. It's understandable, but sad. My realization that I was different came about as a teenager.

Teenage Torments

I had gone from a laid-back middle school, which had both boys and girls, to a conservative high school, which was all boys. It was a shock to be in thrown into this testosterone-charged environment, especially because organized sports became a huge focus. At my middle school, I had not needed to worry about being on a team. My English middle school didn't really emphasize team sports so it never became an issue.

In high school, I hated all sports with a passion, and found the fact that we were supposed to compete against each other in activities (including cross-country running in the middle of winter) ridiculous! So, I was fortunate to find comfort with a group of boys in this new world who almost hated exercise as much as I did. I liked hanging out with them in school, complaining about playing rugby in the rain or doing gymnastics in the freezing gym. Out of school, I liked being with them doing the kind of things that boys like doing—apart from sports—such as seeing James Bond movies, eating Wimpey burgers (the English equivalent to McDonald's at the time), and watching *Lost in Space*.

Whereas the boys I chose as my friends weren't into physical exertion, they weren't into mental gymnastics either. In fact, a couple of them didn't want to be in school at all, rebelled, and got into trouble. As a result, they were hauled up in front of the principal and mocked for being bad and stupid.

I had been at the top of the class at my middle school. At my high school, I found that I was concerned with fitting in with my new sports-loathing buddies. I didn't work hard academically so I got Cs rather than As. When my teacher saw my results he was very disappointed and said, "At this school, you're supposed to be the cream of the crop but in your case you're beginning to curdle." It is interesting looking back that I so wanted to fit in with a group—any group—that I was willing to take the wrath of my teacher and get poor grades rather than fulfill my true potential.

Choosing to fit in with a group is a choice that we make as kids. We decide that we would prefer to be part of an outsider group rather than being ourselves and taking the chance that we will be alone. We'll see in Chapter 4 how crucial these decisions are.

Making a decision to not be ourselves so that we can fit in is a decision that we often make. We give up something we are good at, a passion, people we care about, or dreams we've treasured because someone or something tells us that being different is wrong and being alone is forbidden. What a strange world and a sad society where that has become the commonly accepted message. Many people evaluate themselves, find that they are different, and don't like what they find. We need to say no to compromising our true nature just to fit in, and say yes to being okay with our uniqueness. Acceptance is the key.

Being Different on the World Stage

Being different is fine. In fact, it is more than fine. It is fabulous. Thomas Quasthoff is recognized as one of the finest bass-baritones in the world. He also was a thalidomide baby, which resulted in his stunted growth. He acknowledges his difference, but the main thing that one notices in his performance or television appearances is the joy he finds in singing and his love of music, be it Mahler or Miles Davis. This is how he described his first recital:

> *The audience did, in fact, whisper and look rather dumb-founded... But as soon as my baritone rolled through...there was silence in the auditorium. It soon became amazement, and by the end it was sheer enthusiasm.*
> —"Thomas Quasthoff: A Mighty 'Voice' Soars" by Tom Huizenga
> Talk of the Nation, NPR.org
> Quoted from "The Voice: Thomas Quasthoff"

His parents initially put him into a group home because it was believed that he couldn't cope with being in a regular school. He was cautioned against being a musician and instead studied law. Yet he still believed in his singing ability. He took private lessons and became a professional singer. He never performed in an opera because he felt his appearance would be too distracting for the audience. In 2003, however, he was cast as Don Fernando in Beethoven's Fidelio. Don Fernando, a powerful government minister, saves the day and the life of the hero in this opera with a happy ending. Quasthoff is truly an inspiration to all of us. But outsiders have been inspiring throughout the ages.

Being Different About the World

Nicolaus Copernicus asserted that the Earth rotated on its axis once a day and traveled around the sun once a year. At the time, astronomers believed that the Earth was fixed and the rest of the universe revolved around it. In the 16th century Copernicus's theory was considered wacky. He was an outsider. He took 30 years to publish his theory, partly because he was a perfectionist but also because he was worried about what the Church might say. The Church believed that the Earth and man were at the center of the world, and to come up with a different view was sacrilegious. Copernicus is now considered the father of modern astronomy.

Here is Copernicus's bold defense of his outsider ideas:

If perchance there should be foolish speakers who...should dare to assail this my work, they are of no importance to me, to such an extent do I despise their judgment as rash.
—Translation as quoted in *The Gradual Acceptance of the Copernican Theory of the Universe* (1917) by Dorothy Stimson, p. 115

I want to be alone

Greta Garbo is ranked as the fifth most important female film star ever by the American Film Institute. She was also a Swedish immigrant, who had to leave school at age 14 when her father died. She talked about how it felt after signing a contract to go and work in Hollywood:

People here do not know what it means to my people when somebody goes to America. There is always much crying—a feeling that they will never come back to their own country and their own people.
—*The Story of Greta Garbo as Told by Her to Ruth Biery*. Photoplay. April, 1928

After making it in the United States she gave up her career when she was 36 initially as a temporary retirement but eventually as full time. In her later life, she became a recluse, living outside of Hollywood in New York. Even though she did not appear in movies, or give interviews or write about her life, she still was a sought-after celebrity. Unlike some of her contemporaries who stopped working and slipped out of sight and mind she was still in the spotlight although she always tried to avoid it.

The first disabled president

Franklin D. Roosevelt is the only U.S. president elected for four terms. A Democrat born into an extremely wealthy and established family, he was responsible for the New Deal, which provided relief, recovery, and reform to turn around the Great Depression. Yet he also had polio and spent most of his time in a wheelchair, although he avoided being seen in public using it. At the time, a disabled politician was almost unheard of, but he did not let that define him.

He was also married to his cousin, had affairs throughout his career, and yet continued with his marriage even though he and his wife kept separate households. In the America of the time, this too was sufficient reason to be seen as an outsider. Finally, he was a supporter and promoter of civil rights, which was not a popular stand at the time, another reason to be an unsuccessful misfit. Even in this historical position on human rights, things are not clear-cut. Roosevelt was also accused of not doing enough to save holocaust victims and of being responsible for the internment (imprisonment) of U.S. citizens who were of Japanese, German, and Italian descent.

Yet as we look at his life and career, he is remembered not for his flaws and challenges, but his successes. An outsider for his times, he was both a successful force in wartime and peacetime and is recognized as one of the most influential leaders of the 20th century.

We are trying to construct a more inclusive society. We are going to make a country in which no one is left out.
—Franklin D. Roosevelt

We just liked ice cream

Two guys named Ben Cohen and Jerry Greenfield made a fortune selling ice cream with names like Chunky Monkey and Cherry Garcia. Before that, Ben studied pottery and jewelry-making and was a cashier at McDonald's, a Pinkerton guard, a night mopper at a couple of supermarkets, and an assistant superintendent at the Gaslight Square Apartments. Jerry applied to medical school twice but was rejected, and as a hobby swallowed fire. They started their business—for fun!

Ben and I met in junior high school. We actually went to the same temple and were in Sunday school together as well. After less than stellar college careers—I was trying to go to medical school and never got in and Ben had dropped out of college—we just decided to do something fun. And since we'd always liked to eat, we thought we'd do something with food and we chose homemade ice cream.
—*One Sweet Whirled,* Stefanie Pervos, associate editor, JUF News

Published by Jewish United Fund/Jewish Federation of Metropolitan Chicago, Reproduced with Permission, *www.juf.org/news/local. aspx?id=43816#*

Ben and Jerry are also socially conscious and environmentally aware. They embraced this progressive position at a time when few businesses were talking about being "green" or doing the "right thing." A potentially suicidal step at the time, it led to more notoriety, public awareness, and resulting success.

The company tries to get involved in certain issues. One thing the company has done, it has pledged not to use bovine growth hormones in the products and puts a message on all our packaging. The company has taken a stand about the military budget and trying to find nonviolent, nonmilitary solutions to conflicts. I think one interesting thing is that the business will be outspoken about issues that are not necessarily in its financial self-interest. Ben & Jerry's has always felt that we should be standing up for issues for the good of society and not just to make the company more money.
—*One Sweet Whirled,* Stefanie Pervos

They are also both Jewish, which can, even in the 21st century, result in being considered an outsider.

I think my Jewish background made me aware of people that were discriminated against, and that a big part of the issue is poverty and people not getting their fair share of social services because of discrimination. So in terms of the stands Ben & Jerry's has taken, it has been about trying to get more fair treatment for people who have been discriminated against or exploited.

They led their company until they sold it in 2000. They are lovable outsiders and ethical successes.

Everyone Loves a Lesbian?

Ellen Degeneres started out as a stand-up comic. She had her own sitcom and then came out of the closet as a real-life lesbian on her television show. At that time, she didn't fit in to the TV network's view of what a good show should be about, and she didn't match many viewers' idea of what a star of a show should be like. Although her coming-out episode was one of the highest rated of the show, the series did not continue that success. Her show was canceled and she went back on the comedy club circuit where she continued her success being a comedian despite her rarity as a lesbian comic.

> *You have to have funny faces and words, you can't just have words. It is a powerful thing, and I think that's why it's hard for people to imagine that women can do that, be that powerful.*
> —Ellen DeGeneres, *US Magazine*, January 1995

But she soon reappeared on television hosting awards shows. She got high praise for hosting the Emmy Awards in 2001 after it had been cancelled twice due to the tragedies of 9/11. The entertainment industry was concerned that it would seem crass to be celebrating artistic achievement after the horrors of the terrorist attack. Ellen pulled it off. She connected with viewers, focused on achievements, and was respectful of the recent events. She summed up her successful outsider status in this line that she delivered at the Oscars:

> *We're told to go on living our lives as usual, because to do otherwise is to let the terrorists win, and really, what would upset*

the Taliban more than a homosexual woman wearing a suit in front of a room full of Jews?
—Ellen DeGeneres, Emmys, November 2001
http://en.wikipedia.org/wiki/Ellen_DeGeneres

She then went on to gain more success with her own talk show. In 2003, her show received 12 Daytime Emmy nominations, more than any other talk show in the history of the Daytime Emmys, and won four Emmy Awards. As an outsider comic she fit right in to daytime television promoting a "negative-free zone" as the theme for her show.

> *For me, it's that I contributed.... That I'm on this planet doing some good and making people happy. That's to me the most important thing, that my hour of television is positive and upbeat and an antidote for all the negative stuff going on in life.*
—Ellen DeGeneres

Everyday Outsiders are Inspiring, Too

Outsiders are also, and most often, average people. I meet them every day and, through my coaching and training people, I am inspired to see outsiders transform into successes before my very eyes.

Designing Success

A client and good friend of mine, Jana Rosenblatt, a costume and production designer, also used her talents to become a successful outsider. She was good at her job but was having trouble finding work in the ever-changing entertainment industry. She needed some other work. She was flamboyant, colorful, and theatrical. She didn't fit in to the corporate world, and she didn't want to put her creativity aside for a paycheck.

She was used to creating costumes and sets for big movies and small theater productions. In her career, she had been creative, flexible, and able to work under extreme time constraints. Her work had required great organizational skill, an ability to produce costumes and sets extremely quickly, and the ability to manage a tight budget.

She used her design and organizational skills to create a successful interior design business. Further, she leveraged her ability to work under tight deadlines by making that one of her unique selling points. She furnished a home for a recently divorced man in a matter of days, and readied a house for rental in an equally short time. People loved her services.

> *For me, leaving the work force of a company and starting my own business was the best thing I could have done. I am self motivated and I need to be an integral part of my projects. In my capacity as a freelance interior designer I can establish the "rules" of the game with my clients. I can educate them on how best to use my time so that they have the benefit of my experience and I am in the right place and the right time to move the process forward. That is to say, it is easier to invite myself to meetings when I am my own boss....*
> —Jana Rosenblatt, JanaDesign, Los Angeles, California

Here is another example of how an outsider became an insider.

Hippie Engineer Morphs to Creativity Consultant

"Maxine" wasn't a "regular" engineer at the Middle American, conservative engineering company where she worked in research. She was eccentric, wore hippie clothing, talked about the Tarot, and had been married five times. She had managed to hide out for years in research—picking up a paycheck but never getting promoted or recognized for her contribution because, frankly, a lot of people thought she was nuts!

But a recession hit and layoffs struck the company. Maxine was worried. With talk of cost-cutting measures in the air she realized that her future wasn't certain. At first, she decided to try to fit in more. She could change her look, stop reading Tarot cards at lunchtime, and not talk about her last husband or her latest boyfriend.

But then she thought about her plan. If she tried to act like a regular engineer she would be like all the rest of the engineers. She liked to be different and her gut told her that being different was the way to be successful.

She realized that if she tried to be like the other engineers in the company she would never win and might be one of the first to be laid off. So she decided to be herself. Maxine was very interested in creativity. As an engineer she didn't just dabble, she studied systematically. She had studied the science behind creativity in depth. She saw that creativity and problem-solving could be useful in her work. She started to solve problems in different ways and was surprised at the success she achieved. She learned to develop lateral thinking and to come up with breakthrough ideas. She had an unusual skill that added to her workplace value.

How to make her company see beyond her hippie clothing? She began to develop her interest into a training program. She had noticed that many of the engineers had trouble thinking out of the box. This led to the company missing opportunities and failing to come up with innovative new products and services. Her coworkers, her boss, and other executives in the company noticed what was happening.

She offered the training program to a group of friends at her company. They loved the training and talked about it to their buddies and their bosses. Maxine was asked to teach the class again. And again. And again.

Employees loved the course and wanted more. They learned how to be creative when solving problems or designing new products. Maxine loved teaching it. She could be as wacky as she wanted. That was the point of the class. She turned her weak point into her strength.

Her company was facing competition in the global market, and while her colleagues were being laid off, she kept her job as creativity czar. She had converted from outsider to successful outsider.

The Unique U Principles

Outsider? Successful outsider? What makes the difference? I believe it is what I call the Unique U Principles. These are the principles that unsuccessful outsiders can use to become successful at work and in their personal lives. Time and time again, I have seen these principles work well with my coaching clients. They have also helped me go from surviving to succeeding. Simply said, these are the key drivers that enable you to go from being different and unwanted or out of place, to unique and in demand.

- Exaggerate Your Eccentricities.
- Master Yourself.
- Be Bold and Big, Not Bland and Boring.
- Find Your Release in Relocation.

Let's look at each one and see how they can create success.

Exaggerate your eccentricities

I went to the University of Wales in Cardiff, which had a number of colleges within the university system, and the one I went to was the Institute of Science and Technology. Not surprisingly, many of the students were scientists and technology specialists and especially engineering majors. I was pursuing an English and Communication degree. Whereas there were hundreds of engineering students, there were only 15 of us "arts types" in our year.

We all lived in the dorms where we could have hidden out and ignored the would-be engineers. They were the majority, and it would have made more sense to have kept our heads down and run a low profile. But my friends were not used to down-playing who they are—especially when it came to having fun.

Although my friends are now successful and solid members of the community, respectively a financial controller (Andy), lawyer (Steve), senior civil servant (Trevor) and technical writer (Julie), they were then and still are somewhat eccentric. If you are being kind, this translates to being different; if you, not it translates to weird. The engineers were not kind in their translation.

Now this may be a generalization, but engineers, and especially young male ones, have two hobbies: One hobby is drinking beer, and the other hobby is drinking beer. So not surprisingly, one of the largest societies in the university was the Real Ale Society. Real Ale doesn't mean that there is also Imaginary Ale, but instead means that this is natural, not factory-produced, beer.

Drunken engineers weren't our idea of fun. We wanted to do something different. We also were aware that the university gave the official societies money for administration and resources, such as the use of a minivan. We did not see why the Real Ale Society should get money and our real needs should not.

So we decided to start our own society. Because our group consisted of a bunch of eccentrics we thought we should start an old fashioned gentleman's club (gentlewomen were on equal footing) where outsiders, misfits, and mavericks could hang out. This was long before John McCain and Sarah Palin co-opted the term.

We modeled our idea on British, specifically London, clubs, not U.S. clubs, which I have heard are more like strip joints! London clubs include the Caledonian Club, which requires tracing direct Scottish descent or "having the closest association with Scotland"; the Travellers Club—yes, that is the correct spelling—which requires members to have traveled at least 500 miles outside of the British Isles; and, the Reform Club, which requires that members agree with the Reform Act of 1832 which brought in sweeping voting reforms and created the modern election system. We liked these clubs, which appealed to our high-minded notion of reliving a gracious age.

In terms of class definition it was more Monty Python than Moneyed Classes. The mission of the club was to have fun and avoid drinking beer. More specifically, the mission was to revisit 18th- and 19th-century architectural follies. These buildings were part of the romantic period in England when aristocrats created fantastic estates. Follies were towers built for no purpose, ruined temples constructed as curiosities, and caverns dug out of hillsides to be inhabited by hermits. We also planned to have eccentrics come and speak to our society about unconventional topics, and to hold parties where the gentlemen and gentleladies could enjoy each other's company in a civilized and non-beer drinking environment.

It was a wacky idea—and it worked! The students were intrigued. It was something different. It was making us even more different than we were. Lots of students signed up. Instead of spending time in the Economic Society discussing economics, or in the Politics Society discussing politics, or at the Real Ale Society discussing beer, they could go and drink Pimms (an alcoholic fruit cocktail served by vicars on lawns in Agatha Christie novels), visit 18th-century pet cemeteries, or listen to celebrities such as Michael Palin (comedian, writer, and actor, of Monty Python fame) and Irene Wigglesworth (our friend Andy's grandmother).

Within a year, the Gentleman's Club (okay, so the title doesn't translate so well in these more politically correct times) was one of the largest in the university, with a thousand members. We were outsiders, but successful ones.

Master yourself

After leaving my job as a trainer in London with Arthur Andersen, I was sure that I would never work for them again. Strangely enough, three years later, I was asked to work for them again. During my first stint with them, I had become friends with one of the other instructional designers and trainers, Ross. He called me out of the blue to come and work at the company's training center in Chicago. I was asked to work on a project for three weeks. Once again, I was being asked to write training for accountants, and I was worried that this was going to be another disaster waiting to happen. But England was in the midst of a recession. I had been laid off from my job and had started a freelance career that was taking a dive. Unfortunately, my freelance clients were suffering from the bad economic times and weren't hiring consultants.

I had two choices: I could take this contract or I could face no work, no savings, and foreclosure on my flat in London's Notting Hill. I opted for the easy choice: take the money. But I also knew that I would have to be myself in this new role. I couldn't try to be someone different. I would have to take the consequences, whatever they were!

In the United States, things were better than I could have ever imagined. I was put on a project team with a great group of people from around the world. I was working on a fun training course about communication skills. My boss liked what I wrote. When I came up with ideas for program activities, they were recognized as good. I was valued for my global perspective. I was even praised for my humor.

As part of one of the training projects, we created a video program to explain the cut-off date—in taking an inventory, there must be a cut-off date for sales and purchases. This may mean that all traffic in and out of a factory is stopped while counting takes place, which ensures that transactions are accounted for in the correct time period.

I spiced up this concept with an amusing cartoon character. "Charlie Cut Off," a bendy kind of guy who explained the importance of the concept. The video got good reviews and proved to be an effective learning tool.

I was rewarded for my creative work with an extension of my contract from three weeks to six weeks, and then six weeks to six months. I was recognized as someone different and valuable by being given my own office and inclusion in key strategic projects.

I knew things were different when I was complimented on my socks—a rather bright red—by my boss. At a meeting, he said that my socks were outstanding. At first I thought he was being sarcastic, that he was an American version of my UK boss with his fashion views of my career-limiting tie. But my U.S. boss was serious. I stood out compared to some of my more corporate colleagues, but this seemed to be okay. In fact, it turned out to be a plus. Through mastering myself I had become a successful outsider.

And so my love affair with America began. Today, I am now a successful outsider with dual citizenship in the U.S. and the UK.

Be bold and big, not bland and boring

I was still working in Chicago for Arthur Andersen, two years after my initial three-week project had started, and life was good. I knew I was a successful outsider because I was trusted with bigger projects and increasingly strategic tasks. When I was selected to work on a high-level project, which was going to educate the company about how to use the Internet effectively, I knew that I had been selected for my creativity.

I was part of a team that produced a live broadcast television program that was produced by Arthur Andersen's own television studio. The firm had invested in its own private broadcasting system that allowed the company to broadcast to all its employees in its offices around the United States. The system also had the technology to interact with the audience. We could talk to individuals, and viewers could e-mail or fax in questions.

This was in the late 1980s and the Internet was not new but was not as widely used as it now. The Internet began to become popular in mid 1990s. At this time technophobia was running rampant. There were partners at the firm who never read e-mail, consultants who told clients not to e-mail but to call, and a general fear of the technology among important groups of people. My group was directed to educate and communicate to the firm how to use the Internet effectively in business, and to answer some frequently asked questions.

The audience for this program was an intelligent but fact-focused group of professionals. When I say *professionals*, it would be more accurate to say a large group of consultants and an even larger group of accountants. It would be easy to say that accountants are dull and unimaginative and that the only buzz they get is from accounting procedures updates. But that's a stereotype.

The thing about stereotypes is that sometimes there's a grain of truth in them. Our audience was used to doing things in a very traditional way. The firm had bought in to a private broadcasting system but was not using it imaginatively. The usual television broadcast program would consist of a bunch of experts seated around a bunch of artificial flowers discussing a bunch of worthy topics. It wasn't always the most stimulating entertainment, was certainly not prime time, and was only slightly better than Public Access TV.

The firm had an important message to communicate to its employees, to make sure that it was done effectively, decided that something different was necessary. I was known for being different, so doing "something different" meant bringing me into the picture.

In addition to myself, a fully certified square peg, the team consisted of a producer, Julie Brown, and a technical expert, Cindy St. Ores, both of whom were unique in their own way. The producer had an extensive collection of chicken memorabilia, and, continuing the poultry theme, the technical expert in a previous career as a flight attendant had demonstrated the safety belt procedure on a rubber chicken way before Southwest Airlines encouraged a sense of play with their staff. So we were three outsiders.

The program's purpose was to educate the employees about the Internet. The Internet was still not widely used and even less understood.

The team came up with the concept of driving on the Information Superhighway, or more particularly, taking a taxicab on the Information Superhighway. Cindy, the technical expert, of rubber chicken fame, was the cab driver. I was the hapless traveler, who got lost on the Super-highway and who had to take a cab to get home. It was a match made in heaven. Our producer, Julie, was the wonder woman who made it all come together and enabled us to look good and be successful outsiders.

We had a fake cab, with real footage behind us, just like old Lucy shows when they took a road trip. The cab bounced up and down like an old car might as it hit bumps and holes in the road. A bunch of burly grips—the people who move things around on a film set or a stage—bounced us up and down in the car. It was really fun, and I had a blast.

Okay, you may say that the only award this program should win is for program mostly likely to fail. Well you would be wrong. The firm had the technology to have the audience interact with the presenters of the program, so we ran contests and call-in promotions, and there was a lot of irreverent play. The response was positive. People weren't tuning out halfway through the broadcast but were engaged and participating.

We had created something very different from the normal round-peg type of broadcast, which was a traditional talking-head, presentational style and program.

We only realized how different it was when we were selected for an award. The program received Best Program Produced by a Private Network—a national prize and a big deal. At a very fancy awards dinner we received our plaque. It was pretty unimpressive looking, but it was a good feeling to be a winner, considering we were all square pegs, all outsiders. This was a first in my career.

Find your release in relocation

Corinne, the cosmopolitan linguist and excellent English teacher, shipped out to the suburbs and became a success too. She came to real-ize that she was in the wrong place. She loved being with people from other cultures. Having been born in Latin America, and having attended school in Europe and America, she was happiest with people from all around the world, not just from the south side of Chicago. Her reloca-tion release was realizing that she was not happy in that location. Her coworkers had grown up in the suburbs, most had not traveled abroad and tended to be conservative in choice of activities for fun. They were nice people but she did not have much in common with them. It made her sad and depressed.

Corinne also saw that she was wasting her language abilities in the current job writing training programs to be delivered in America. Her global perspective, her foreign language ability, and her cultural awareness were not needed. She also missed teaching and being with students from other countries. She felt like an unsuccessful outsider in both her work and home situation.

So Corinne started to explore opportunities in other locations using the contacts she had made teaching English. She talked to people, networked extensively, and landed a job in her favorite city—Paris. She transferred within the same company to France.

In the new job, she was doing some instructional design along with a lot of teaching. In the instructional design work, she had to interact with people from all over Europe. She had to use her cultural perspective to be sure that it was a global program, not just an American one. In the teaching, she was interacting with employees from Europe, Africa, and the Middle East. She loved it!

The work was good and the environment in the office was great. Every day she used her language skills, speaking in French with her coworkers in the office, and Spanish, Italian, and Portuguese with her coworkers in other European offices.

In her home life she also found more satisfaction. She found friends who had lived all over the world and who had experienced many different cultures. They liked ethnic food, foreign films and travel unlike many of her former U.S. colleagues.

In the new location, Corinne had people who understood what she was saying, who appreciated her stories and loved her cooking. She was still an outsider, but her language skills and her cultural sensitivity made her a valuable resource. She was a successful outsider. Kudos came to her recently when she was acknowledged as one of the top performers throughout the European offices of the company. She was a success—period.

3
DISCOVERING YOUR UNIQUENESS

Converting outsider qualities into a successful job or self-employment opportunity is the subject of this chapter. We are going to look at what you have to offer as uniquely qualified outsiders, how those elements can be translated into viable options, and how your oddball triumphs can also point to a potential new career path. Let's start with what you have to offer as an outsider. How do you discover your uniqueness?

Let's Start at the Very Beginning

So where to start? I have found that the most obvious place to start is at the beginning. And for me the beginning is when we didn't have any mortgages, mates, or mind-trips to work through. We were all just having a good time being kids.

I always loved to write stories when I was a child. I loved to make people laugh. And I was a very good listener. I spent a lot of time with adults and learned to hear what was being said and what was not being said. It's not surprising that I ended up as a coach and writer. I have also found that my coaching clients had often discovered their passion back when they were small.

We can get a clue if we go back to our childhood, our school life, or our first work experiences. We were often enthusiastic and excited about what was possible. Kids want to be firemen. Students want to change the world. Interns want to know how to get to the top.

But we often get worn down as we find that we're not valued and respected. What we thought was important turns out to be unimportant to our professors or bosses. We give up. We decide to settle. We accept being an unsuccessful outsider.

Projects to Paint

One of my clients, "Ella," also found her uniqueness when she revisited her youth after struggling with a career that did not feel right to her anymore.

Ella was a successful outsider project manager who rediscovered her passion for building and designing houses when she remembered how much she loved repairing and building things with her father when she was young. After successfully remodeling her own house, she started a business helping customers build their dreams by renovating old homes. Just as Ella connected her childhood dreams with her present occupation, you can evaluate your current career goals with your childhood fantasies.

Once you know what makes you tick—your positive and negative misfit or outsider qualities—then you can start to work on what products or services you can offer to an employer, client, or customer.

Choose to Listen to Your Heart

Deep down is where you will find some of your best answers. That is, if you choose to listen. Sometimes, we keep so busy that we never have time to listen to our hearts. If you're unhappy it's easier to work hard, collect your salary, and enjoy your free time 110 percent than to dwell on what makes you unhappy. But if you stop and reflect on your differences, you will start to see a glimmer of light that will illuminate a possible future. You will remember what you like doing, what you love, and what is part of your soul. It may be hard to focus on things you really like, those you know are not part of your current life, but it is the gold in the dirt. Stop and listen. This story shows how finding your uniqueness may take time and inspiration.

"I think I'm going to be a nurse," I declared, after months of trying to figure out exactly what I could do that would not involve college and would hand over a paycheck from the get-go. I was lucky in that I had grown up in a country (Ireland) that endorsed the idea of a practical training with only eight weeks in the classroom per year. The rest of the time I would be tenderly holding sippy cups to old darlings who would pat me on the head and tell me I was wonderful. Little did I know.

My rude awakening to the school of nursing was to be told that I could not wear pants in the classroom (nurses' uniforms at that time were restricted to dresses—there were no pants even though they were common with women outside of nursing). My next horror was the sight of an F on my first weekly test. Things only went downhill from there. For three years I fudged my way through cleaning sluices and washing body parts until I had my "staff nurse" belt.

Inside me there was a healing gift, and through the years of working among the sick I developed the knack of knowing the right thing to say to them. I was able to warn visitors of a relative's bad turn before they walked through the door. I could prepare a man emotionally for surgery. I could cajole and chastise. I could pray. Inside me was the healing gift of counseling.
—Sally Hanan, former nurse, writer and counselor, Austin, Texas

Be Present to What's in Your Present to Find Your Joy

If you are still stuck then think about your current life as an adult. What are your hobbies? What interests you? What voluntary work do you do and love? How do you spend off-time with your family, friends, or coworkers? Often you will spend time away from work doing what you really like, and this may be connected to what makes you different. Do you love to doodle during meetings? This may be a clue!

A friend of mine gave up a corporate career she hated after she realized that she got a big kick out of cooking. She felt like a misfit talking about investments because she didn't find it "real." Making her grandmother's recipes was practical, tangible, and real! She went to cooking school where she could develop her differences into a new career.

Be a Detective to Find Your Sweet Spot

For those of us who are more practical than spiritual, you may find that you get inspiration from doing some detective work. Look at other successful misfits for ideas. Dean Koontz, a famous writer, used his unique view of life—he doesn't fly, prefers to hang out with artisans, than celebrities, and had his multi–million dollar house built by the guy who put in his swimming pool and had never constructed a house before—to create wild and exciting characters that his readers love.

> *Books saved his sanity as a child, he says, and possibly "saved me from turning to alcohol the way my father did to try to escape."*
> —Murray Waldren interview with Dean Koontz, *The Australian*
> *http://copywriter.typepad.com/copywriter/2005/01/dean_koontz_int.html*

Koontz loved horror and sci-fi. He began writing as a youngster even selling some of his writing to his family. He credits reading to saving his life and his career success.

> *...maybe there's some other person...who will see something in your books that will illuminate a little bit about life for them...*
> —Murray Waldren interview with Dean Koontz, The Australian
> *http://copywriter.typepad.com/copywriter/2005/01/dean_koontz_int.html*

Read magazines and newspapers, watch movies, television, and plays, visit museums and galleries for ideas about how to turn your misfit qualities into a job or a business. Learn from other people, your boss, or your kids to get more insight on your products and services.

Don't censor yourself. You may come up with an idea to sell the greeting cards that you love to make, but may also decide that it will not pay your bills and so discard the idea. At this point be open. You may be able to have a dual track—a job and a small business. You may be able to work with someone to create a business that will support you. Or, simply, you may not know what you don't know—that is, you don't have all the information yet. Maybe Hallmark is looking for the next unique range, of cards and your cards, which celebrate ancient festivals such as Midsummer or All Souls Day, are just what they are looking for.

If you get a feeling, go with it. If you see a coincidence, note it. If you get a warm glow when you talk about an idea, keep working at it! Use your intuition to find the misfit services and products. Above all, don't be scared. Remember: No action equals no pain *and* no pleasure, but action gives you *possibility*.

What do Other People See in You?

Explore what other people see in you. I love working with coaching clients because I get to see the shining success the client is often too shy, modest, or unaware to recognize and promote. I am working with a wonderful woman who has both a strong spiritual and artistic flair but also a solid business brain. What a fabulous combination for success. We worked on a consulting business for her. She can go to the heart of an issue, and then, because of her analytical ability, present it in a meaningful way. Her love of art and beauty means that she can also connect with those people working in that world—artists, writers, performers—who may struggle with the business part of their lives.

Perception process

A good technique to uncover these skills is to use a **Perception Process.** This is where you ask someone you know well to give his/her perceptions of you—your personality, your skills, your knowledge, your attitude—both the positive and those that are less effective. This person can be someone you know well—a family member, a friend, or a coworker—or someone you don't know well. Surprisingly, you sometimes learn more from someone you don't know well than from someone you do.

The process is for you to sit and listen to the other person give his or her perceptions of you. You must resist the temptation to "facilitate" it so that he or she covers both negatives and positives, or can "answer" your questions, or gets to say what you want to hear. It is also important not to agree or disagree with the person's thoughts and opinions. It is certainly not a time to argue. Your job is to simply listen, make notes, and take in the information from which you may learn. If you let the person talk freely, you will find that he or she will open up and be honest in his or her feedback. You will often hear some really heartwarming descriptions of you—which may surprise you. That's great information. These positive qualities may be the unique qualities that make you stand out. You may also hear some negative comments. There are three things you can do with the more challenging feedback.

You can reject it. The feedback does not resonate with you, and this may be because of previous judgments the person has about you or because of his or her own hangups. This can be especially true of people who "know" you well. They may base some of their comments on old stories that are not helpful. It's good to have warning bells go off when your cranky aunt starts saying, "Of course your generation had always has a problem with taking responsibility for looking after their family." Keep smiling but know that this is probably not helpful!

You can accept it. The feedback does give you some insight into who you are. It does make sense and it's something you want to work on. However, beware! Sometimes people will say things that support your own doubts and fears. You may be actually reinforcing some of your limiting beliefs. Watch out for red flags such as, "Well you always say that you're not good with details." The question to ask yourself and others would be, Is that true? What evidence do you have for that? Are you really worse with details than other people, or are you holding yourself to an impossible standard?

You can analyze and research it. You might hear something which surprises or shocks you but doesn't sound wrong or right. This is the time to do a little exploration. You may want to make a note of it and ask someone else or a number of people what they think of the data. Avoid asking them if it is right or wrong but instead get them to comment on it. For example, someone might say during the process, "You sometimes seem like you don't want to be successful. You had that great idea for a book but then you seemed to lose interest in it. I thought that was a pity." Now you might agree, "Yes, I did drop the book," and not agree, "But it doesn't mean I won't come back to it next year when I'm done with school." So you might ask a friend, "I was wondering what comes to mind when you think of me and you think of successes?" This is a more open-ended way of getting to the question, "Do you think I avoid success?" You may learn a valuable lesson from the information you get during this process.

Thinking outside the box or at least taking unorthodox approaches may make your outsider qualities work to your advantage. There is a Russian problem-solving technique, TRIZ, that does just that. With 40 principles it looks at creative ways of solving technical problems, but has also been successfully used on non-technical issues. For example, "13, the other way round—invert the action(s) used to solve the problem (for example, instead of cooling an object, heat it)." (*www.triz40.com/aff_Principles.htm*)

And how could we apply that to ourselves? Maybe we have always done work that pays well and now we could try work that doesn't pay well or even volunteer work. This could be a breakthrough. We might find that the work we choose when we don't focus only on the money is rewarding and fulfilling.

We've looked at things you loved as a kid, things you are good at, and things that other people notice about you. Now it's time to organize that information and make sense of it! You want to be able to use the data to position yourself as an empowered outsider and get to that successful and fulfilling career. We want to explore and determine what are our viable options.

Ways of Looking at Uniqueness

We can look at our uniqueness in various ways:

- **Skills**—what you can do: speak French, program in C++, or ride a unicycle.
- **Knowledge**—what you know: all the names of the seven dwarves, how a tractor engine works, or how to make a perfect muffin every time.
- **Behaviors**—what you do: easily give honest and motivating feedback to others, smile when you meet new people, or love to solve problems.
- **Experience**—what you've done: worked in a bakery in Paris, worked in a bakery making wedding cakes, been a wedding planner in Las Vegas.
- **Attitude**—how you do things: with a smile, with purpose, treat everyone as if they were a trusted friend.
- **Personality**—how you present yourself: sunny and bright, cool and collected, or serious and studious?

Work through your skills, knowledge, and so on so you can convert your uniqueness to a product or service.

Sometimes it helps to see your future through another person. Work with a friend, family member, coworker, or coach to discover some of your future goals. Sometimes we are scared of our power, or we don't want to be creative, to imagine what could be, because we would become more acutely aware of how little we are settling for today. That's when another person can help us to think big, and embrace what is possible, rather than living in a small world of restriction because that seems safer.

In this "And then what?" exercise, you will work with a partner in imagining your future. The partner encourages and motivates you by asking certain open-ended questions that are designed to help outsiders think bigger. Once the partner has an answer to your question, he or she asks you another question. The partner should use probing or clarifying questions to get to the heart of the issue.

For example, Jane is an assistant for a law firm. She doesn't like the work much and thinks there is more to her future than doing administration.

She feels as though she doesn't fit in. She has an artistic flair, and this causes people to comment negatively about her. Her flair comes out in a colorful clothes and the way she decorates her cubicle. Her boss thinks she should blend in to the background more. He is worried about upsetting clients. Read her conversation with a friend as the partner asks her about the future.

Partner: Tell me about how you are going to go from an outsider to a successful insider:

Jane: I'm going to look at what I'm good at and work from there.

Partner: What are you good at?

Jane: I don't know. I guess I'm good at design.

Partner: Are the other assistants good at design too?

Jane: No, most of administrative assistants like me in my office aren't.

Partner: Who needs that design work in your department?

Jane: Marketing wants these graphics. And the senior partners for their presentations. I always do those for them. I'm really the only person who can do graphics in the office.

Partner: What does that make you?

Jane: Unique. I guess I'm unique.

Partner: Maybe you can get them to create a design position for you at the office.

Jane: Maybe. I always had an idea for greeting cards.

Partner: Great. That's something you might be able to start out at home selling them online.

Jane: I'm going to talk to my boss about creating a graphic designer role for me and I'm going to look into online businesses.

Bingo! Jane has figured out what makes her unique. You can use the same technique to talk about your future career.

What is Jane's product or service?

Jane could sell herself as someone who knows the store (knowledge), understands computers (knowledge and skills), and loves to teach (behavior and attitude). She is a scarce commodity—there will not be many people who have store knowledge, want to train, and have the teaching experience.

Analyze You!

Reflect on what makes you unique from the analysis of yourself. What do you know? What is your personality? What experience do you have?

We have part of the puzzle. We know what we can offer. We know what our product or our service is. But this is only half the story. We also need to know who wants to buy that product or service. Let's look at an example to see how both sides of the equation come together—the services or products on one side and the buyer on the other side. In this case the buyer is the employer, client, or customer.

My analysis

Let's analyze why I was successful working in Chicago for the financial consulting firm, and in London a disaster. Which of my "services" sold and which ones bombed? We'll start off with why the equation didn't work; why the services I had were not what the buyer (the employer) wanted.

Ten years ago, when I still lived in London, I was excited to get a job as a trainer and technical writer with a large consulting company. I had recently taken a postgraduate course and wanted to use my new skills. I interviewed and nailed the position unlike some of my colleagues that had graduated from the course but still didn't have a job. I was also going to be earning about 20 percent more than a lot of my friends. It seemed that I had landed on my feet with this job.

My new job was one of the best examples you can get of a square peg in a round hole. I was an artsy (English major), liberal (not even a social conservative), creative type who wanted to write, preferably for television, film, or theater. I had a talent for writing and for training. I loved humor and I wanted people to have a good time. The service I was offering was my skill with writing, my knowledge of English, my attitude (being a liberal) and my personality (being a funny guy).

But was the service that I could offer really what the high-powered, conservative, financially driven company wanted?

I would soon find out. I ended up working in Arthur Andersen designing training for their tax division. Before that time, the only thing I knew about tax was that it was the bit missing from my pay each month, and that my parents, who ran a hotel, used to complain to their accountant about how the quarters didn't seem to be three months apart and that they couldn't be due to pay any more tax. I found tax to be taxing!

Despite my doubts about working for a consulting company, I thought it would be a good move. It wasn't writing for TV, but I was still going to be writing. I had been teaching before this and I knew that education and training weren't a bad second choice for a career. Writing training manuals and training videos wasn't bad, even though it wasn't the same as writing for *ER* or *Desperate Housewives*. I thought that my services were going to be well received by my employer.

We know my job wasn't a success. I was looking for somewhere to be creative. The company was looking for someone who was good with administration. They wanted someone who could take care of details and be sure training manuals were produced correctly and that training classes started and finished on time. It was a match made in hell. My downfall was version control. Version control, for the uninitiated, is when you go through various drafts of a book and you make sure that you know which draft is which. You always want your reviewers working on the latest draft. You always want to be editing your current draft. You always want to have your up-to-date draft ready and available. Sounds easy, but I still wake up at night screaming "version control!"

The training went through review after review and each time somebody made a comment, it was added to the most current version. The key words are "the most current version." Unfortunately, I never seemed to figure out what the most current version was.

My attention-to-detail skills were poor. I tried to sell my creative services by designing whimsical and way-out graphics for overhead slides to support the hours of presentation on tax. Mostly these were rejected as not fitting in with the culture. The equation didn't work. What I had to sell wasn't what the employer was buying, and what the employer wanted to buy wasn't a service I could offer. It was taxing for me as a square peg in a tight round hole.

I can still picture my office, with the desk, bookshelves, and floor covered with printouts of the training manual. I would search through the stacks for hours to find "new page A-1-b revised 12/1" and never find it even after intense prayer and talking to a psychic at the equivalent of $1.50 a minute.

The rest is history. The lesson I learned was that I wasn't good with details. Wrong lesson. The lesson I should have learned was how I could use my square peggedness, or being different, to my advantage.

As we saw, just three years after working at this firm in London I went to its Chicago office where I was a big success. Why was that? I was the same person I had been three years earlier. Once again I was being asked to write technical training, not for tax professionals but for accountants. The change wasn't significant in my future success. I was still a misfit.

What was the difference?

Why was my being an outsider an advantage in the United States and a disadvantage in the UK?

The **first plus** was that I wasn't from the United States. I was working on training materials that were designed to be used throughout the world. I am British and I have lived and worked in Asia so I could understand the global perspective. I was an international square peg, and the financial consulting firm was happy to pay 50 percent more than I had been paid in the UK and throw in a car and apartment for my services. The equation worked well.

The **second plus** was that I was a creative writer who also wrote comedy and drama for TV, film, and theater. Unlike my colleagues, I didn't have a Master's and PhD in Instructional Design—how to design and write training—but I did have ideas, creativity, and wackiness from my repressed dreams. I was a creative square peg. The firm respected my ability to bring a new way of looking at things. They even increased my hourly rate.

The lesson I had learned three years earlier was that I wasn't good with details. The lesson I learned now was that I *was* good with ideas. This was the right lesson. I learned how my being an outsider, or a square peg in a round hole, could be valuable. I had an equation that worked well. It's all about reframing.

Reframing for Focus and Fame!

Once we've accepted that we don't fit in, we need to analyze what makes us different. We need to find out how our skill, knowledge, behavior, experience, attitude, or personality makes us different. We then need to think how that can be converted to a service or product. Then the equation comes into play. We must look at our current employer, a future employer, client, or customers to determine what they need.

At first we may not see how our being different can become a product or service. But brainstorming, lateral thinking, creative problem-solving, or working with other misfits, a coach, and a mentor can help you to understand how you can use your differences to make something concrete that will sell.

After we have our product or service, we again may struggle to find an employer who wants what we have to offer, a client who wants to take a risk on us, or a customer who wants to buy this new product or service. Again, it may take time to come up with an answer. Problem-solving can take time, and you may need to enlist some support as you figure out who wants to buy what you have to offer.

It is also vital to be sure that you have a positive service or product as well as a positive employer or customer. A negative product will probably be hard to sell. A negative employer will probably not be someone with whom you want to work. Sometimes what starts negative turns positive, as in this example about a Generation Y employee interacting with a boss from another generation.

> *Isabel was a recent college grad and just joined our company. I invited her to join on a client meeting so she could see how they run. However, I told her to just observe and not say a word. She had a difficult time keeping quiet and when one of my clients looked her way she began talking about an idea that evidently surfaced while the meeting was taking place. I gave her a look of "you are so fired," but to my surprise the clients loved what she had to say and wanted to incorporate her idea.*
> —Kristen Lutz, advertising executive, advertising industry
> Nicole Lipkin & April Perrymore, *Y in the Workplace*, Career Press

For example, let's say you are very scattered at your workplace. You decide that you should work for a company that is unstructured. You can offer you services—being able to work in a chaotic environment—to the employer. Sounds good, but do you really want to work for a disorganized employer? Being an unstructured company may mean it is artistic and creative, or it may mean it is bad at business, or on the way out without enough people to run the business. Even if you discover that the unstructured company is unstructured because it is artistic and creative, do you really want to work for a company that may be so disorganized that it doesn't make payments on time, including your salary, gets bad credit through poor financial acumen, and takes the company into bankruptcy because of bad practices? The answer will no doubt be "no, I don't want to work for a chaotic company even if that matches my own style."

My cosmopolitan linguist friend, Corinne, soon realized she was different. It was then a journey to decide how she could use her unique skills to get a job she loved. At first she kept looking at using her skills in the same environment but she kept running into roadblocks. She kept working on improving her skills, trying to fit in with her coworkers, but she didn't find a demand for what she could offer. No one she worked with appreciated her unique background and expertise.

She gave it some thought, brainstormed with friends, and worked with a coach. She soon began to see that she needed to move to a new location where she would be valued. Through mentors she found an opportunity with the same company, but in Europe. She moved to Paris and became an international successful outsider working for a group of countries throughout Europe, Africa, and the Middle East.

I love the environment. In fact, I'm not sure I could ever work for a single country any more—it would seem too provincial. People get set in their ways and are not aware or interested in the fact that others might see things very differently, or have different needs, sense of humor, of hierarchy, of history, etc. In some sense, If I worked for a single country I'd be afraid that others would be too comfortable, set in their ways and unwilling or unable to listen to others and adapt. Because I've always

*been a bit of an outsider—no matter where I am—that would
bother me.*
—Corinne, Manager, Professional Services Company, Paris, France

My television writer friend realized that she was different from the average writer. She was depressed and unable to see a way out of it until she realized that she had a gift for writing and unique material to work from.

Through talking to mentors—experienced writers in the business—and to fellow writers in writers groups she began to see how her uniqueness might help her.

Her diversity could be a selling point. There were producers who wanted her services—her unique point of view in her writing. She also found that organizations such as the Writer's Guild were trying to increase diversity in the industry. They wanted to help people similar to my friend through programs and competitions. She got on a show as a writer because of her talent and her unique background.

List everything that makes you different, from your clothes to your opinions. Now decide which of these differences could be positive and which would be negative. For example, having bad breath is not likely to be a positive. Being a liberal could be a positive (but maybe not if you are working for a Republican). If you are not sure what makes you different, then ask a friend or coworker. Having an honest and open conversation may be painful at first, but it will be incredibly useful in your future life.

For example, I have a friend who is a talented administrative assistant in the entertainment business. She has worked on television shows, on film sets, and with celebrities, but hasn't been able to find a job recently. She believes that the problem is that she is 50 years old and is a misfit in the business, which is knee deep in 20-year-olds.

Her age is a factor, but more importantly she is a misfit because of her attitude. She sees fault in people and situations. She is a misfit because she is so negative. This is not going to help her get a job. Although I have raised this issue, she doesn't want to hear it. Until she is open to understanding why she is a misfit she will never be able to become a successful misfit.

A person who dresses as if he or she has just come off the set of the Beatles' *Yellow Submarine* will probably fail in a conservative corporate environment, but they may fit well in a retro clothing store and may be very successful.

Finding your different and turning it into a saleable commodity can be tough. There are no guarantees, but we can look for trends, learn from previous experiences, and talk to our coaches and mentors. We must work both with what employers or clients want, and what we can offer.

I failed working for the financial consulting firm in London because what I had to offer didn't match what they needed. The firm wanted someone who was good with details, and who could coordinate and organize training events. I am a big-picture person who loves to create training events, not make the coffee show up at the break on time!

I was successful working for Arthur Andersen in Chicago because what I had to offer totally matched what the company needed. The firm wanted someone with an international perspective. I had lived in Asia and Europe and could bring that unique insight to the training it was developing. The firm wanted someone who could create training and who understood that things were different in other parts of the world!

THE OUTSIDER'S JOURNEY: ACCEPTING YOURSELF AND OTHERS

At some point in our lives, at work, at school, or at home, we realize that we are different. We then make a huge leap. Instead of accepting that we are not the same as other people, we decide that being different is bad. We decide that we should be like other people. We see pain in being an outsider and pleasure in fitting in. We don't accept ourselves. And if we don't value ourselves, then others are less likely to. It's hard to educate others if you don't believe in the message you are delivering!

> *High self-esteem is our birthright. It is the core spirit inside of us. We do not need to pass a battery of humiliating tests to attain it. We need only to drop the thinking that prevents it. We need to get out of its way and let it shine, in ourselves and in others.*
> —Scott Richardson, *101 Ways to Motivate Others*, Career Press

Listen to Your Parents—or Not!

Denise was one of my clients. She was very successful in the entertainment field as a production coordinator, working long hours and earning serious money making sure TV programs got made according to schedule, budget, and the whims of the talent and suits. But she hated it. She did not feel part of the frat boys' club that was the production team. Her dream was to be an artist. She was a frustrated sculptor but she could not accept that, or the success she had achieved. She only saw she did not fit in and was an outsider.

After I worked with her, she began to recognize that the internal voices that told her that she had to be sensible, secure, and sure of herself in her old age were her parents' voices. As a child she had learned that being an artist without stability, a regular income, or pension was a bad choice. Now she began to realize that she did not have to believe that old story. She accepted that she was different. And after working with me she made this statement:

> After meeting with you, I can now say today, no matter what I do for work or how I earn money to live, I proudly can say that I am an Artist and an Educator. That is what I believe in and what makes my heart sing. I am feeling more grounded in who I truly am. So I am on this journey.

—Denise, Artist, Independent, Los Angeles, California

Internal and External

Acceptance is about the internal and the external. There are practices, which work on the spiritual, emotional, and mental levels, and exercises, tasks, and goals, which work on the real-world level. Acceptance begins with us; we can only help people accept who we are once we have accepted ourselves.

Internal acceptance

There are many paths to internal acceptance. Deep down I am okay, you are okay, and the world is okay. There is something bigger than all of us—love, God, a power, Buddha, nature, or whatever we might call it—that trumps our worries and concerns. That is our anchor that makes it okay to accept ourselves.

I have been laid off three times, had major money issues, and difficult times, but there has always been something that kept me going that was bigger than me. Sometimes it was simply a sunny fall day, or friends calling to say hello, or an opportunity that popped up out of the blue when I least expected it. I may not be rich, or have the same amount of hair as I had when I was 20, or have perfect days without a care in the world, but life is pretty good. And when it's not, I do my best to learn and grow.

> *As a successful artist known around the world for my drawings and sculptures of dancers as well as for numerous articles on art and art business, I must work with photographers, models, other designers, and architects.*
>
> *The good part about me is that I have great passion, great enthusiasm, boundless energy, endless creativity and total focus. The bad part is that in my desire to create the best art, the best photos, the best whatever—I drive people crazy. I work them until they drop. I keep the model trying until she hits the exact pose I am looking for. I have the photographers shooting until their cameras explode.*
>
> *So it is not unusual to have people walk out on me, curse me, cry. However, those who do finish a project with me all say the same thing—you drove me crazy, but we turned out the best work that I have ever done. Amazingly, most come back for more. In fact, I have photographers and models waiting in line to work with me, because despite my somewhat trying personality, we do great art together.*
>
> *Accepting myself just came naturally. I knew that God made me who I was and was confident that it was for a reason.*

—Pablo Solomon, artist and designer, Austin, Texas
Pablosolomon.com

Four principles for gaining self-acceptance:
1. Stop the chatter.
2. We are all the same.
3. Give and receive.
4. True passion.

Stop the Chatter

Being different kept my voices busy. This is the internal chatter, those "gremlins," as a coach I know calls them. Simply stated, they are my fears. And they always had some opinion, warning, or comment about my differences. My life was like watching a movie with the director's commentary turned on.

It went something like this:

Okay, in this scene I'm meeting a group of people I've never met. I am taller than all of them so I'm going to be a real outsider.

That person is staring at me and wondering how tall I am.

Why don't you take this direction: slouch a little and make yourself a little shorter! That way you won't stand out so much.

It was irritating and depressing. Eventually, I learned to clear my mind by taking a series of steps.

First, I identified some of these voices. By realizing that there was someone who was telling me to "blend in to the background" I could start to act differently. It's a simple as the idea of knowing your enemy.

I thanked the voices for their concern but assured them that I could manage well without them. The voices are often a part of your subconscious that wants to protect you. They want to make sure you are okay, just like your mother may have when you were small. Just as parents often do things with the best intentions, so do our voices. So don't disown your parents for trying to do the best for you and don't banish your voices without thanking them for their efforts. Just the way our moms and dads appreciate being treated nicely much more than being shouted at, so do our voices!

I monitored the voices. If I found that if I was confused or depressed I thought about what my voices were doing. Were they busy commenting? And was this why I was having a hard time? Or was there something different happening? The voices try to get back into the foreground, to dominate, when you don't notice it.

I accepted that my voices might always be there but that I didn't need to let them decide my life. I could turn them off, or turn the volume down, or even switch channels!

Keeping the chatter down has helped me to focus on what is important—living in the present—rather than worrying about what has already happened.

We Are All the Same

If we believe that we're all part of the same world, created by a universal power, and we're a reflection of that power, perfection, and purpose—then it becomes hard to think that we are worse or better than other people. Of course on the surface there are hundreds of differences, but underneath we're all just energy, souls, and love, however we might want to describe it. If we want to see things in more concrete terms, we're all a bunch of cells, a bag of skin, and a mix of genetic matter. If we are the same on a fundamental level, then how can we ever be outsiders? On the surface we may appear to be, but down deep we are the same and remembering that improves our outlook.

As part of my New Age journey, I attended a men's retreat. It was held in the English countryside in a rundown house with organic food and bad plumbing. Out of the 20 men on the retreat there was one person who literally scared me. John had Hell's Angels tattoos and vicious piercings, and he smelled bad. He was from a tough part of London and I was a soft middle-class suburban type. I decided I didn't like him, didn't approve of him, and was going to steer clear of him.

One of the activities was to work with a partner on key events in our lives that had brought us to where we were. I found myself partnered with this man and discovered that I was completely wrong about him. He turned out to be a gentle, thoughtful, intelligent, and wonderful human being. Underneath the smoking, boozing, and raging that I had seen was a really nice guy. We were much more alike than we were different. From that day on, I learned to see beyond the outside cover of people and read the book inside.

Give and Receive

Many New Age theories advocate some form of giving and receiving as a universal truth. I know that what I give to other people directly relates to what I receive. This can mean physical objects or money, and it can mean actions, behaviors, and words.

I know that if I get to the car rental desk with an "attitude" because my flight was late or my luggage was lost, I am more likely to get attitude back from the person at the counter. If I can get past these issues and approach with a smile and a willingness to understand that she or he may make close to minimum wage and would rather be home watching *American Idol* than trying to understand what the guy with the thick British accent is saying then I am more likely to encounter a friendly and helpful car rental clerk.

Of course we can't always be happy and full of fun, but if we constantly radiate negative feelings it is harder for other people to help us. I have a couple of friends who've each been unemployed for nearly two years. They are both older, and each is a kind of outsider in his own way. At first, I gave them contacts for jobs and freelance work but then I stopped. Although it was understandable for them to be depressed, the negativity that I seemed to get when I offered any advice or support —"That's not going to work," "I already tried that," "At my age I can't," or "I'm not working for that amount of money"—made me decide to give up. I was receiving too much resistance in response to my help, so I gave up. It's unfortunate, but now if I see a suitable job opportunity for them I am most likely going to ignore it. They are sending out bad feelings and now they are receiving the results of those.

If we believe we're outsiders and communicate that to people we meet, then chances are that we'll receive the feedback that we are indeed outsiders. If we say we're failures people will often believe us. Strangely enough, if we say we're successes then the same people will often believe us just as strongly.

A good friend of mine, Paul, is an expert in computer networks. He's also a little eccentric with his hobbies and ideas. He chooses to give people ammunition to make him an outsider—and an unsuccessful one at that. He can be very friendly, has a good heart, and is kind to animals, children, and seniors. But he will say things that push people away. I watched him spend most of one evening discussing how he doesn't need people because he has the Internet. The people who were with him labeled him an outsider. He failed to see that his statement was illogical because he had just spent an enjoyable time discussing interesting ideas with a group of people. He chose to give the group an impression that highlighted his negative views, which aren't really his truth, rather than his positives.

True Passion

It all comes down to passion. Passion is the fire inside you. It's what motivates you to bounce out of bed early in the morning. It makes you cry, laugh, sing with joy, or scream with anger. The spiritual practices my clients follow all lead to a fire in themselves. It leads them to these questions:

- "What do I care about?"
- "What is important to me?"
- "What makes me happy to be alive?"

Passion will never lead to these thoughts.
- "What do other people want from me?"
- "What makes me a good boy or girl?"
- "What would look good on my resume?"

Passion is the elixir of life. Take the time to reflect on what is important to you. Remember your dreams so you can analyze them and find out what's on your mind. Draw on your subconscious for clues about what really makes you tick. Throughout my journey I found out I was passionate about writing, food, travel, and my friends. I saw how my passion drives me forward.

The successful outsider doesn't have to work at being who he or she is. If you are passionate about your beliefs, nothing is false. You can truly enjoy yourself.

An artist known for being an outsider puts it this way:

...Accepting myself just came naturally. I knew that God made me who I was and was confident that it was for a reason. I also knew that accomplishment, creativity, having life's adventures, etc. was more important to me that what others thought about me.
—Pablo Solomon, artist and designer, Austin, Texas
www.PabloSolomon.com

A friend of mine is a successful executive, managing a division for a large company. He is great with people. He does a good job. He makes an impressive salary. However, he always wants to do something creative, something different. He always wanted to work in the media. But he was brought up in a family that told him his responsibility was to provide for his family. His parents certainly didn't want him to be miserable, and he wanted to please his parents. This set up a real dilemma for him.

Management is not his passion. He has to work really hard to be good. He works long hours. He gets stressed. He is afraid that one day someone will realize that he is not in the right job. He does a good job of disguising who he is, but it comes with a price. He gets tired. He gets sick. He cannot enjoy his free time because he is always worrying about his work life. It's sad.

Spirituality as a Tool for Inner Acceptance

The first part of the acceptance equation is the spiritual side. By reading, taking classes, and experiencing new sensations we gain acceptance and become comfortable with being an outsider. Some of the key steps in the journey, as we've seen, are understanding the stories we often create, seeing that what we give is often what we receive, and understanding the power of passion.

Meditation can be a key part of this journey. There are many other ways to get there. It is important to create a practice such that you do something regularly. Meditation does not only mean sitting quietly alone for an extended period of time; it can also mean taking a few minutes while stuck in traffic to focus on your breath. Small, consistent steps are a great help and lead to bigger and better steps down the road.

It is essential to have support and a community to help you with your spiritual journey. I have a wonderful coach who helps me with my spiritual practice. When the voices start shouting each other down, Kathryn Christy helps me to quiet them. Being among loving, positive, or like-minded friends is a great support.

The spiritual steps are vital but I also believe that we must take practical steps to accept that we are different. These are the external steps that, combined with the internal steps, produce the total equation for self-acceptance.

External Acceptance

To really accept who we are, I found that we have to:

- Seize our life.
- Find mentors.
- Work with coaches.
- Take action.

Seize your life

It is possible to spend much of our time reacting to other people and their views and not living our lives. If we're always trying to please other people we don't have any time left to be ourselves, to accept that we are who we are, and that, on some level we don't fit in. The time spent on worrying about our friends, family, and their opinions is wasteful at best, and painful at worst. John Adams found himself seizing his life after a work strike gave him the space to think about what he really wanted.

> *As the PATCO Air Traffic Controller's strike commenced I found myself wanting it not to end, at least not until I got our business off the ground. Then I realized that I wouldn't return if we were called back to work. I was soaring in a new mysterious world of business and the vision of creating something from nothing began to get bigger and brighter.*
>
> *I was discovering that my wild scattered mind with all of its dreams and eccentric ideas was not abnormal but the stuff of which entrepreneurs are made. I had felt like an outcast from the "tribe" and now I felt like the Chief; yes, Chief Cleaner, but more than that, the Chief Architect of a new company.*
>
> *I accepted myself for being radically different and encouraged others to do the same by embracing their unique talents.*
>
> John A. Adams, author, *Miracles at Work: Building Your Business from the Soul Up,* Enfield, Connecticut

Seize your life means living it, converting ideas into action. You can spend a lot of time reflecting on why you're different. You can also spend your time trying not to be different, to fit in to a model based on others' expectations. Or you can move past your doubts and simply enjoy your life. Which will you choose?

Find mentors

Sometimes we forget that we're not the only outsiders in the world. There are many great examples of outsiders currently and historically, famous and unsung, that are blazing the trail for us and setting valuable examples. When we realize that we're not alone, we are not terminally unique, and that we have fellow square pegs, who are a few rungs above us, it adds comfort to accepting who we are.

One of my happiest times was when I was still in London. I had gone to work for a multimedia company that designed training programs. By *multimedia* I mean that the company made programs that used video, computer text and images to produce content for large companies and organizations.

The company was full of square pegs like me. The employees were all about the same age, had traveled or lived abroad, and tended to be creative rather than analytical. Most people who worked there felt uncomfortable in a suit, and if they had to wear one for a client meeting, they would choose a tie guaranteed to be different. There was no such thing as a career-limiting tie in this company. In fact, the only career-limiting tie was the one you wore if a client wasn't present in the office. There was no such thing as "business casual Fridays"; at my new company we had "really casual all week." My managers were mentors.

I learned from my mentors that people valued my creative skills, my humor, and my wacky ideas. I began to accept that I was an outsider and grew to love it. I saw that being an outsider was a plus, a differentiator that could lead me to greater success.

I created a sales training program for a financial institution that had a soap opera theme. One team created another retail training program that incorporated a contest. It was so popular that employees had to be limited on how much time they spent on it! One of my colleagues worked on a training program about communication that had a murder mystery as its central theme. It was fun.

I felt very at home there, enjoyed the work, and slept exceptionally well at night. Had the company had not been hit by a recession, I probably would still be working there today.

Having mentors taught me that there was another way of living and working that offered joy and fulfillment, and this enabled me to accept who I was.

Work with coaches

Coaches and *mentors* are sometimes used interchangeably. I see a difference. Mentors are people who are often in the same field as you but are a couple of rungs higher up the ladder. They have achieved more than you in their particular field. If you work hard, and earn their confidence, mentors give advice about how to make progress in your career based on their own knowledge and experience. The mentor doesn't get paid for his or her help, but is rewarded by knowing that he or she is developing the next group of leaders. Many are "giving back" from having received mentoring from their seniors at similar stages of their career.

Coaches often don't have particular expertise in the same field as you, but have the skills, knowledge, attitude, and experience to help you create solutions to problems and strategies for success. I have coached senior marketing vice presidents, but I don't have a marketing background and have not been a senior VP. My skill is to be an expert on careers, a strategic thinker, an objective sounding board, an idealist and a realist, a motivator, and a champion for my client and his or her career.

I was working with a coaching client who is a senior vice president, makes nearly half a million dollars a year, and is well respected in the healthcare industry. Although I don't have the same experience or title as her, my broad coaching experience and objectivity enabled me to effectively help her with outsider issues. She had been given some feedback that in meetings she was too quiet and needed to speak up more. She is somewhat of an outsider among the group of men she works with. They are loud, opinionated, and always ready to verbally fight out differences.

My client was devastated by the feedback. She questioned who she was, what she was doing, and her success. I worked with her to see that she was different from her colleagues, but that was okay. I helped her to see the great achievements she had made, supported her in getting positive feedback from her reports, her peers, and her bosses, and helped her develop the ability to see herself and career objectively. Through the coaching process she came to accept who she was, and to value her tremendous contribution to the organization.

Take action

Taking action is sometimes the best path to accepting that you are an outsider. Some wait for that magic moment when we're happy with the world, and all is in perfect alignment, before making changes or taking action. Too late, many people find that magic moment never comes. They have worked on their spiritual side, they have found mentors and coaches, but they overlook the action component and still don't accept they are different. They keep looking for answers, solutions, and quick fixes. Sometimes you just have to throw your hat over the wall and then work on how to get over or around it.

I once attended a New Age course with about 200 other people, including Juan, an interesting man who made films. He was funny, thoughtful, and popular with the other course members. I had written some movie scripts and so I was interested in meeting with him and talking about film.

However, although I can talk to a large class without a problem, I am often quite shy and introverted in the midst of a large group. I sometimes find it hard to go up to people and say hello.

Juan seemed to have no problem networking. He chatted with all kinds of people. I decided that I was an outsider in Juan's easy-going world. For three days I thought about how I could get to know him, how I would bump into him, or how someone I had met in the group would also know him and would introduce us.

The course was nearly at an end when the facilitator introduced a new activity. He asked the course members to go and talk to someone they had not already met. I found that Juan had selected me. We began talking and I was amazed when he said: "I was going to talk to you earlier in the class but you looked like you had a good joke that you didn't want to share. I thought you didn't want to talk to other people in the class and I didn't want you to think that I was an idiot!" I had been worried that I was an outsider in Juan's world and Juan was worried that he was an outsider in mine.

The lesson I learned was, "take action." Instead of worrying about what people are thinking, and whether they will accept you or not, just go and find out. If you take no action you will guarantee your result—no pain, but you will also have no pleasure. Action doesn't assure a safe outcome but it does offer the possibility of good things. Taking action can result in acceptance.

Now that we have looked at how you can accept yourself, we can look at how you can help other people in your work environment accept you.

The Four Outsider Bridge-Building Principles

Life is about compromise. Outsiders may complain that other people don't understand them and blame them for their lack of understanding, but that is not fair. Both the outsider and the insider need to work together to understand each other. In the workplace that can mean that the outsider has to reach out. The following bridge-building principles give you an olive branch of understanding to offer to the insiders with whom you work. By using these principles you can transform what others might perceive as a negative quality into a positive perception.

Outsider bridge-building Principle #1: Let people know that you embrace your uniqueness.

Instead of apologizing for being different or ignoring your outsider differences, embrace them. In fact, celebrate them! Attempting to come off as someone other than yourself is not only emotionally depleting but also futile. Would you rather be the out-of-focus, low-volume, black-and-white you or the color, high-def, 3-D, surround-sound version?

Being British, I had to try to fit in with my American coworkers. I felt uncomfortable around the Fourth of July. I said "great" when I meant "lovely" and I even tried to lose my accent. But eventually I realized that I could never fake being a Yank, a non-Brit. I simply didn't have the same background as my coworkers, and that was that. I embraced who I was, an English-American who was proud of my roots as well as my adopted country.

Understanding what makes you different is the first step. Accepting it is the second step. The third step is to focus on what makes you unique so that you can accentuate it. And the fourth and final step is to make what characterizes you as different your trademark. Be yourself, warts and all, embracing and rejoicing in your differences rather than hiding and denying them.

Sarah, a television writer, who was female, Hispanic, and lacking in contacts, was faced with a white, male, old-boy network. She found success by adhering to Principle #1. After trying unsuccessfully to market scripts for established TV dramas, Sarah made a decision to embrace her outsider quality by writing about a subject she really cared about. She wrote a pilot (the first episode) of a TV show based on an overweight inner-city Latina who is sent to a school for gifted students in the suburbs. Sarah's script reflected her own story of not fitting in as a teenager and she poured her heart into her writing. Her agents weren't happy that she had written the Latina pilot and they wanted her to focus on more commercially viable scripts. But when Sarah was interviewed for a new writing position, she showed the producer her pilot script. He loved it and hired her. Her boss wanted a different voice and a unique perspective. He got both from this successful outsider.

Outsider bridge-building Principle #2: Invite your coworkers to sample your worldview.

When we deny who we are, or pretend to be something we are not, our coworkers may resort to creating stories about us. Often the fictions they invent are more interesting, colorful, and damaging than the truth. Instead of letting our coworkers tell tales about us, we need to set them straight about who we are.

James realized he needed to level with his coworkers after stories started spreading about his slurred speech and wobbly gait. No one he worked with knew what the problem was, but a few creative types fabricated the story that James had a drinking problem. The truth was that he had multiple sclerosis and had been too embarrassed to talk about what made him appear different. When he finally set people straight about his physical problems, James got nothing but support, even from those who had crafted the alcoholic scenario.

By being honest about what makes us different, we can overcome a great deal of workplace stress. And leveling with your colleagues need not entail unnecessary personal detail, conflict, or argument. A simple assertive statement of the truth about who you are can make a big difference in other people's acceptance of you. On the other hand, being passive and saying nothing, or aggressively demanding that people accept you, only further alienates those you seek to win over. Assertively standing up for yourself is true empowerment.

Using Principle #2, Corinne, the cosmopolitan linguist and English teacher whom you met in Chapter 1, became a happily successful outsider. Rather than trying so desperately to fit in with her suburban American coworkers, she began to consider more outsider-friendly opportunities. She "came out" by talking openly to her boss and others in the organization about her passion for languages and foreign cultures. That action was instrumental in leading to that new dream job with the same company in her favorite city, Paris!

Outsider bridge-building Principle #3: Teach people about your eccentricity.

We sometimes expect people to be mind-readers. Although we are different from those around us, the difference may or may not be as obvious as it feels to us, and we sometimes think that somehow others should "get" who we are by some kind of osmosis. Instead, we need to take the time and have the patience to educate other people about what makes us different. Rather than dismissing other people as insensitive, uncaring, or stupid, we need to give them the benefit of the doubt.

A case in point: I took a series of improv classes at Second City in Chicago, which some of my more conservative coworkers found more than a little strange. But when I explained that apart from having fun, it was great training for being in the moment and would help tremendously with my presence and communication style on the job, they began to understand my eccentricity.

By helping others to understand what makes us different, by clearly explaining or demonstrating who we are, we'll be much more likely to bring them around to our side.

Outsider bridge-building Principle #4: Make your uniqueness your trademark.

Outsiders who don't sound, look, or act like other people can use their difference to their benefit by turning it into their personal "brand."

Labels can be derogatory or limiting, but they also can be helpful if they enable people to quickly and accurately understand a product— you. Rather than waiting for other people to label us, we can beat them at their own game and label ourselves in an honest and positive light.

A coaching client, Teresa, is a fabulously talented entertainment executive. She has a background in film and television development and has worked at Disney with many famous directors and celebrities. Although these credentials make her a valuable executive, they are not what make her unique. What sets Teresa apart is her love of musical theater and her ability to perform. She was brought up loving musicals, and from an early age was passionate about performing. Such interests and talents are unusual in a film or television executive.

For many years, musicals were out of fashion at Hollywood studios, so Teresa's love of this genre was an untapped resource professionally. Her passion for musicals was an outsider quality that had never contributed to her success, until several blockbuster musicals hit the big screen, including *Moulin Rouge* and *Chicago*. As Teresa looked for a new position in the entertainment business, she used her musical theater background as her unique selling point. Her trademark became: The film and TV executive who is passionate about musical theater, dance routines, and belting out showstoppers. Teresa successfully used what previously had pegged her as an outsider to succeed as a one-of-a-kind entertainment exec whose time had arrived.

5

MARKETING YOUR UNIQUENESS

Just as companies market their products or services to customers, so, too, must outsiders market their unique qualities, skills, and experience to a prospective employer, client, or customer. Based on previous experience, many outsiders might believe that marketing yourself is a waste of time. It is easy to assume that round pegs, or insiders, view us square-peg outsiders as annoying anomalies that need to be altered to fit in, or thrown out as rejects—but that is not so. We are valuable and valued. It comes down to one simple factor: Opposites attract!

Trust the Process

Here's a story that exemplifies how adversity leads to advantage, and why being valued as an outsider in one workplace does not mean that you won't be highly valued in another.

While attending graduate school, I was working as research associate and was fired. Losing my ability to pay for schooling, I had to leave grad school. My displeased boss viewed me as a very disorganized employee.

A friend and former neighbor encouraged me to visit the University of New Mexico. There, I learned about a position in the medical research wing for which I had a unique skill. I knew how to operate a device called an Elutriator.

I managed to get that job, and within nine months' time I had developed two different ways to isolate and grow Type II lung epithelial cells. One method made use of the Elutriator, and the second method involved use of standard tissue culture techniques. I had used those same techniques in the prior job that I had lost.
—Dr. Sue Ellen Chehrenegar, freelance writer, Culver City, Calif.

We can see how Sue fitted in one job and not in another. For her first boss she was seen as disorganized with the second she was seen as a valuable contributor. She marketed her skills with a particular device and that was what got her the job. With the first job it wasn't enough. This is sales in a nutshell. There is rejection. And salespeople know the process—the more you hear no, the nearer you are to a yes.

Opposites Attract

The grass is greener on the other side of the fence. Meaning that insiders secretly want to experience what it feels like to be an outsider? Well, perhaps that's too strong. Insiders don't really want *be* square pegs; that would be too weird. But they are curious; the unknown tempts them.

So what are the poor round pegs going to do? Pay up for a square peg to give them a glimpse of the other side, a vicarious thrill, to bring some color, some life, into the workplace. In a nutshell, that is one of the keys to marketing yourself as an outsider—offering something that the consumer doesn't have and realizes that he or she wants!

Managers and clients know that they want something different, something out of the ordinary. Whether it is a customer service rep, software programmer, or salesperson, the boss may have tried the usual and now wants the unusual. Logic dictates: *If what you are doing isn't working, try something—or someone—different.*

That's where you come in. Smart managers value diverse perspectives for better problem-solving and product development. They want different personalities and sales techniques for broader customer reach. They may not know what they want, but they realize more of the same isn't going to produce desired results. It is up to us outsiders to help insiders understand that we offer the solution.

When I worked in the training department of a large company, we found that people got tired of all the training we threw out at them. The director of the department knew that they often didn't bother to watch the video or manual we sent. I knew we needed something different so I pitched the idea of creating a video in which we played into the idea that this was "yet another training program." I was on camera complaining about the training department and how they bombarded the employees with training. This shock treatment worked. Employees did watch the program because they were so surprised to see someone say what they had been thinking. The satire worked and the program was a success.

Four Principles of Marketing

So how do you market yourself as an outsider? Where do you begin? In the following Four Principles of Marketing, you can see how they apply equally to your strategy as an outsider. Here they are:

1. Product
2. Pricing
3. Promotion
4. Placement

We'll look at each element and find out how they apply to your journey from outsider to highly successful outsider.

1. Product

The successful sale can be described as meeting the needs of the employer, client, or customer. First, we need to establish what those needs are, and then we have to present our services in a way that clearly shows that we can meet the employer's or customer's needs. This is our outsider's "product." Some products (or services) will exceed an employer's or customer's wildest dreams, and some won't. You don't sell a hammer to a customer who needs a screwdriver. The customer may not know what he needs; it may be up to you to make that determination, and once you do it is also up to you package the screwdriver in a way that distinguishes it as the best screwdriver on the market.

Product exceeds expectations

A friend of mine is Chinese, bilingual in Mandarin and English, and once worked in an advertising agency. She was the only person in the office with this cultural background and language skill. She was also the only non-white employee, had a heavy accent, and her Chinese-bought wardrobe sometimes stood out as different. But this was back in the 1980s before China became an economic power. China's commerce with the West was still in its infancy and few Westerners knew much about doing business there. All this worked in her favor. Her product—the ability to speak Mandarin and understand Chinese culture—was a huge plus. Her firm was looking to expand its business and she suggested doing ad campaigns for Chinese organizations. Her bosses saw the potential, and that they needed her skills to be successful. Her product was a great match for the employer's needs.

Product does not meet expectations

That was a good example of how an outsider's product exceeded expectations, but it's also important to look at products that didn't exceed or even meet expectations and to understand why they didn't work.

I once managed a project for which I had a great outsider working on the team. He was a great graphic designer, with exceptionally high standards, and he produced beautiful and perfect work. His background was interesting: He had traveled to Europe, was into fine art and ethnic cuisine, and dressed fashionably. He did not fit in to the company. The other graphic designers in that department did not have his level of fine arts training, nor did they know about foreign travel, much less food.

In general, they were much more concerned about how they could get a presentation turned around as quickly as possible than how stylish and cutting-edge it could look.

Unfortunately for him, the other graphic designers had a better handle on what the company really needed than did my star graphic designer. The company's client was not into beauty and perfection! The client was a financial company with a practical and focused view of results. They primarily wanted a fast turnaround. They liked excellent quality and creative design when it suited their needs and timetable, but they would sacrifice those preferences to meet the deadline. If it was a choice between a dull but on-time design of a new logo, and a cutting-edge design that came in late, they would choose the timely option every time.

One time we were asked to produce a concept for a logo. The designer did his best work, putting in many hours. The client didn't like the look and rejected the idea. The designer had spent too long on something that was not going to be valued. We both learned that we had to be deliberate in meeting and exceeding the client needs, however the client defined them.

Repackaging an outsider product for major success

The following story shows how Belle Chen took an outsider product, destined for failure, and repositioned it for major success. It didn't happen overnight, but she was accepting and aware of her outsider gifts, and realized early on she needed to develop a strategy to capitalize. The repackaging strategy she used is what I often coach my clients to follow.

I have been working in big FMCG (Fast Moving Consumer Goods) for more than 10 years in Asia. It's a fast-paced business and you gotta move fast to beat the competition. At the age of 28, I joined a leading European healthcare company as a senior manager who had five direct reports and more than 100 indirect reports. Traditionally this position required a pharmacology graduate because you need to be able to communicate well with pharmacists and doctors. I had my MBA and a bare minimum of medical knowledge. Half of my direct reports had graduated with a pharmacology degree. And they were known to be proud of their degree. I was unqualified in the eyes of my big new team

for two reasons. I was younger than them, a lot younger than some, with less industry experience, and I didn't know medical science or terminology.
—Belle Chen, general manager, 360 Jewels, Placentia, California
www.360jewels.com

Faced with this challenge, Belle decided to offer her outsider perspective as her value-added product. She skillfully worked with the insiders in her department to understand and fulfill their needs.

On a day-to-day basis, I asked and listened a lot. I gave them my opinion from a "strategic point of view" and asked for their "technical point of view." And, together with my team, we came up with an integrated and effective strategy. They felt respected, involved, and important. They were also impressed by my different approach. They said for a person from a different field, I quickly understood the medical field and offered loads of big-picture ideas. I gained more respect, trust, and teamwork as time went by.

Although on the face of it, the job was not a match, Belle turned a negative situation into a positive one by building on her strengths and repositioning her role to give the employer a "product" that worked well.

2. Pricing

How do you sell yourself for top dollar? When will you not be able to command top dollar? What determines the difference between success and failure in pricing?

As part of the sales process you set the price for how much you or your products are worth. This depends on what the going market price is, how your product is distinguished from the norm, and the ability of the customer to pay.

If you not only meet the customer needs but also exceed them, you can be sure of getting the job, contract, or sale, as well as the pay, fee, or price that you want. If you only meet the needs then you have less ability to negotiate what you want in terms of pay, benefits, or price.

For example, when I first started consulting in Chicago 15 years ago, $50 was the going rate an hour; I earned $65. I received a 30-percent premium because I had international experience, foreign language skills, and a global perspective. The client saw the value, needed that skill set, and was able to pay. Perfect!

Supply and demand: my friend with the Mandarin language skills negotiated herself a hefty pay increase and promotion. She did very well and was able to reduce her hours, increase her vacation, and take stock options. She was a scarce resource in demand and could negotiate a package that worked for her.

3. Promotion

Promotion is about how people get to know about you. The foundation of promotion is having a brand. When we market our outsider qualities we need to know what brand we embody. Under the Promotion Principle, you can establish your personal brand with four personal brand strategies.

Strategy 1: Market your unique outsider attributes that are scarce.

Strategy 2: Bring a new twist to something old.

Strategy 3: Create something as unique as you are.

Strategy 4: Satisfy a customer's, client's, or employer's desire.

Strategy 1: Market your unique outsider attributes that are scarce.

It is simple: Do you have something that other people want? When I worked in Chicago, my unique selling point was my global expertise. I had lived in Europe and Asia, spoke other languages, and had worked on international projects. I was developing training materials that were designed to be taught to 5,000 people around the world.

Sports stars who have exceptional talent are also a scarce commodity. They don't need to fit in. They can dye their hair pink, display tattoos all over their body, and even wear wedding dresses (think former basketball star Dennis Rodman) and still be accepted. Their skills outweigh their differences—and the show they put on is a pretty nice bonus.

Your marketing must make your unique selling point clear. A global perspective is part of my pitch to international clients. I give an example of how I once planned a seminar in which the U.S. members of the team scheduled dinner for 6 p.m. As the seminar consisted of 60-percent foreign members, the time didn't work. For southern Europe, 8 or 9 p.m. is customary, while the custom in Latin America is 9, 10, or 11 p.m. We established a compromise where cocktails and hors d'œuvres were served at 6 p.m. and dinner at 8:30 p.m. Everyone was happy.

Strategy 2: Bring a new twist to something old.

Sometimes, it's not that we want to build something new, but rather that we want to give a home we are fond of a facelift or a new coat of paint. In my earlier example, my employer had a formula for training, but wanted to give it a twist. I was the twister they needed.

Unlike my colleagues, I didn't have a Master's and PhD in Instructional Design, but I did have ideas, creativity, and wackiness. My marketing message was that I could take uninteresting material and bring it alive.

Similar to their clients—the accountants—the trainers were focused on facts and figures, making sure that the details were right. I had already found out that wasn't my forte.

This really came home to me when I was part of a team that produced an educational program that was going to be shown to the entire company, through their own private "television" broadcasting system.

The training department had pumped out training videos at regular intervals so prolifically that people were tired of them. My client wanted a different way to train the client on coaching skills, so I suggested we take a satirical approach.

In the video, an "expert" would explain to the audience all about how to coach people they worked with. Instead of a serious approach, it would be a kind of toned-down Monty Python. It started off with the presenter tossing a training department memo into the trash. The video got people's attention. Instead of being another "throwaway," the audience watched, laughed, and learned.

Strategy 3: Create something as unique as you are.

The famous story of 3M and Post-It Notes is a good example of something unique: A scientist was working on a new adhesive, and, as glue, it was a failure. In the range of existing products it was an outsider. But the scientist found that its main failing, that it didn't stick permanently, was actually a huge advantage. The rest is history.

An actress I once coached on career goals was from Europe and had a strong accent. She has been working on sounding like an American, disguising her heritage, as much as possible. She was competing with lots of American actresses for every part. We talked through what made her different and decided that she should use her accent to her advantage. In an audition she would be the only one with a sexy Eastern European persona. It worked. By being her unique self, she got more work than she ever had before. She marketed herself as the actress with the sultry accent.

Strategy 4: Satisfy a customer's, client's, or employer's desire.

This was the strategy for my writing career. I have had a number of books published (in fact the number is seven), not counting this one. My most successful book fits Strategy 4.

George Sees Stars, my most successful book, is a short book written for young students who are learning English as a foreign language. To date, I have sold 80,000 copies. That's pretty good by any measure. Many new novels are lucky if they make their print run of 5,000.

Why is this book successful? Because the reader expects something different and that is what I deliver.

My short story is part of a series. Not just any old series but one of the best-selling series for EFL (English as a Foreign Language) entitled "Streamline," published by Oxford University Press. It doesn't look like a textbook; it looks like a comic book on LSD. Students and teachers expect something different when they buy this course.

And that is what they get. The book has a variety of stories, cartoons, colors, and jokes. It is well researched and a good teaching book, but it is also slightly surreal, wacky, and full of quirks. Kids love it, and, with it, they sometimes forget that they are learning English at school and just start having a good time. I used my outsider qualities to make this book work and meet the customer's expectations.

This is how another outsider, foreign-born Ron Shimony, whom we met in Chapter 1, satisfied the needs of his employer Nextel.

> *I vowed to work hard on myself and stop worrying about what everyone else thought.... The month of January was coming to an end, and a $1,000 commission bonus was on the line. I had to produce total of 50 Nextel phone sales in addition to my quota in order to qualify for the bonus, and I was short 26 phones...*
>
> *I got in my car and drove away to a customer's location to seek new business.... On the way there, my cell phone rang.... How soon can you meet my main guy in Naperville to set up my company with 27 phones?*
>
> *It may be that my hard work was paying off....*
>
> *My momentum going into February was incredible. The hard work I invested in generating referrals started to pay off. In March, an amazing thing happened: I broke the company's sales record for the month.*
>
> —Ron Shimony, speaker and author, Schaumberg, Illinois

In Ron's case his hard work, his faith in himself, and something larger paid off. Simply he stopped letting being an outsider get in the way and just focused on making the insiders happy. And it paid off!

Use all four personal brand strategies

So how would someone apply all four strategies?

A friend of mine is a career coach. She works with a high school district to help its teachers. She is an outsider because she is not a teacher and does not have an educational background. She is a professional coach trained to help people develop their career potential.

She developed this niche and has been quite successful. Instead of competing against other coaches for business clients, she has her own private marketplace and growing niche expertise.

How did she use the four personal brand strategies?

Strategy 1: Market your unique outsider attributes that are scarce.

In an education workplace, there is typically a scarcity of little discussion of career goals. The teachers are just too busy coping with the day to day to spend time on future goals.

Strategy 2: Bring a new twist to something old.

When they do have some free time, experienced teachers will try to help less experienced colleagues. An in-house coach extends a concept that has already worked before, but brings a new twist and added value. The in-house coach has time, can be consistent, and will work with everyone not just selected people.

Strategy 3: Create something as unique as you are.

Coaches in the business world are commonplace. In a school, they are uncommon.

Strategy 4: Satisfy a customer, client, or employer's desire.

This factor does not apply here. If the coach worked in an advertising agency then the coach might have to do lots of creative games, simulations, and visual activities. That audience expects something different from regular coaching.

4. Placement

The fourth Marketing Principle explains how to connect the dots between oneself and one's customer to sell what you have to offer.

Finding customers

We'll look at finding customers in three ways:
1. Looking for a new job.
2. Finding freelance work.
3. Starting a business.

Who would employ you? Who would want an outsider with your qualities? Who would make you a success?

Strangely enough, the first place to look is where you currently work. Susan, whom you met in the first chapter, did exactly that. She wasn't happy being a machine operator where her analytical smarts weren't appreciated, so she found another department where she was highly valued. Initially, she had been an outsider because she asked questions when things went wrong and took responsibility for quality instead of just leaving it to her boss. She found her passion for doing things the right way was an ideal fit for the quality control department. QC needed someone who knew the processes intimately, who could talk to the operators on the floor, and who could be tough about taking action if needed. Susan fitted the job description exactly.

Sometimes the job may be in the same group or department where you already work but taking a different function. Sometimes the job may be the same job but in another division or subsidiary, or it may be a different job in another part of the company. An actor I knew was turned down for a part in a play and ended up directing instead.

Why does it make sense to find a customer in your current employer?

- You are a known quantity.
- You have inside access to explain your outsider services.
- You know who will listen and who won't, and who is most amenable.

Working in the same company means you retain seniority and benefits such as pension rights; you avoid dislocation and keep friends and coworkers you like.

It is important to keep an open mind. When our job sucks, we often decide the whole organization sucks! In fact, if we are happy doing what we are passionate about, we may find that the organization is actually fine. Many outsiders decide that the problem with their work is the company, so they move to another company. Same job—different company—same issues. They decide that they need to work in a small company, not a large company. There, they find the same issues, or, with fewer resources to deal with them, worse. They decide that the problem is Texas so they move to California. The issues are the same. The common factor is those outsiders and their inability to find a role that fits their outsider skills.

Although staying put makes sense, what if you decide that your outsider skills are not well suited to your current industry, company, or organization? Start with your passions. Where would you love to work? What kinds of environments do you like working in? What do you believe in?

One coaching client has gone back to her college roots of activism and is looking at job opportunities within nonprofits rather than her usual corporate suspects. An actress I know, who never felt comfortable in show business, has followed her love of kids, and the future they represent, into a teaching career. A teacher I know analyzed what he liked best in a career and found the answer wasn't education but books. After some training, he pursued a job as a librarian.

Make a hit list of rival companies and companies with whom you would like to work. It includes companies and people you respect, like and admire. A hit list provides an opportunity to be creative. By doing research you will find companies that match your passion and desires.

If you want to work for a company that has on-site daycare, flex hours, sabbaticals, and so on, do some digging, ask your friends, look on the Internet, and yes, you will find a company that has such an environment. You will even find companies that allow you to bring your pets to work so Fido or Fifi can hang with you during the day.

If you want to work in fashion, in politics, or in Tennessee, there will be a company or organization that is ideal for you. List your top target companies and start to find out about them. Who are the key players? Trade associations or conferences? Who are their customers? What are their key products and services? Then use this information to find out more. Ask your friends, coworkers, and contacts who and what they know. There is a certain magic in writing down who you would like to work with and why.

Serendipity: Stack the Odds in Your Favor

I was writing a film script that I thought would be perfect for one of the characters on the hit TV show *Frasier*. I put his name and the show on my hit list. That night I went to my local video store and saw that actor browsing. The next day, I learned that a friend's brother was good friends with the same actor. And a week later I found out that a friend's husband worked for a company owned by another one of the actors in the show. Amazing!

Each person you contact can lead to another piece of information or another person that brings you closer to your goal. The closer the contact, the better the chance it will lead to work. Stack the odds in your favor. If you find a name on the Internet and you send an e-mail cold, your chances are remote compared with connecting directly to someone at the target company, whether that person is the janitor or CEO. If the person you know is a friend who knows you well, your probabilities of success increase. Everyone knows someone, who knows someone, who can help us. Ask!

Working on Your Own

You may also find that you don't want a job, but you want to go freelance. Often we enjoy the work but not the routine, fixed hours, and bureaucratic administration. By becoming a contractor or consultant many of these issues can be removed. You may not fit in to a corporate community because you don't like working 40 hours a week. Turn this to your advantage as a freelancer where you can work less than, and sometimes more than, 40 hours. You may value variety. A client values flexibility.

If you decide to go the freelance track there are different ways of getting customers. I like to think about this in three ways:

1. **Direct to the Client.** ABC company wants a computer programmer and you work for them on a project, contract, hourly, or daily basis. ABC pays you directly, and, because it your client, not your "employer, it does not pay you benefits or deduct tax. You need to find the client, bill them, collect payment and pay your own taxes.

2. **Through an Agency.** There are lots of agencies who will find you work. Instead of ABC paying you directly, XYZ Agency pays you. The agency takes a commission or fee for finding the client. It evaluates your qualifications, finds the client, and often does the billing and collects

the payment. Many freelancers prefer not having to do sales and marketing and will let an agency do that for a fee.

3. **Working for Another Freelancer.** "Pat Consultant" gets really busy and so sometimes Pat needs to get an extra pair of hands. You work for Pat who works for ABC company. Pat got the client and probably Pat invoices and collects the fee. Pat may be generous and not take a commission or Pat may take a percentage of the fee or a fixed fee for finding you some work. This kind of relationship is usually more collaborative and can be more informal than a standard agency relationship.

How do you find clients, agencies, or other freelancers? Again, start off with what you know. Many freelancers find that their first client is their old company. Obviously you know the corporate environment, you have certain knowledge and skills, and you have your outsider qualities. Your frustration with the lack of a creative output in your prior job may make you the perfect person to do a fun project for your old boss or another division. You do what you are good at, and your old company gets someone with whom they have an existing professional relationship!

A friend of mine worked fulltime as a training director. She loved to travel but she found it impossible with her career. She found a freelance role with her company such that she worked for them for six months a year and traveled the rest of the time. The arrangement was a win-win situation all around. Her company didn't want the expense of a high-level fulltime employee. They could pay her to focus on key projects and let someone else at a lower level work on the administration and routine work. My friend knew the organization and the executive team and could be flexible. It was a great match.

Broaden that "hit list" to brainstorm different possibilities. You can also look at the news and current events to help you with your search. A colleague of mine specialized in consulting to companies with workplace diversity issues. If she read that a company had just been sued for discrimination, she contacted them. She was sure that they needed her help and would be willing to pay for it. If a company is laying people off then that may be the perfect time to get some freelance work. I know that sounds strange but it is true! The company has work to do but doesn't want to increase headcount so may consider freelancers who are cheaper and more flexible—sometimes the companies will use people they let go of but more likely is they go to temp agencies or freelancers in the community. If you see that an agency has won a major new account, opened new offices or hired new executives this could be a sign that the agency is expanding and may be taking on new freelancers. Or, sometimes new CEOs will clean house, clear out the "deadwood" and look to bring in new people loyal to themselves. This could be the perfect time for you to introduce yourself.

Joining professional or networking groups is how you can meet other freelancers. By establishing relationships with other like-minded individuals you will find ways that you are able to help each other out. Sometimes to bid on bigger jobs you need to team up and bid as a group—this is a great way to build contacts and win new business. You can also meet other freelancers when working for a client and that can lead to fruitful ventures down the road.

You may be the kind of outsider with a strong entrepreneurial spirit who really wants to run your own business. You have decided that you have the ability to offer a product or a service based on your outsider qualities and now you need to find customers.

Although many times when we go into business we choose a new field, leveraging our experience in an industry we know is typically more profitable and allows us to better evaluate the risk. Your best customer could be your old employer.

The famous true-life con artist Frank Abagnale, Jr., portrayed in the hit movie *Catch Me if You Can*, made a fortune from forging checks. After being released from prison, he made good money legally by consulting for banks who wanted to protect themselves from forgery. His knowledge is crucial.

If it doesn't work to sell services or products to your former employer, you may be able sell to their competitors. A program development executive for a major TV network was asked to research the television market for a rival network when she left her job. She used her TV contacts to research current and future programming needs for her new client.

If your product or service will be sold to your former company or a rival, take a fresh look at the customers who want your product. Those customers may be very similar to you. If that is the case then you need to find people where you hang out. If the customers are not similar to you then you will need to look in different places.

Finding Your Market

For example, let's consider Jane in the previous chapter and where she will find a good market for her skills and qualities. Recall that she works in a clothes store but loves to teach. So she teaches reading to inner city kids, teaches basic car maintenance at a college in the evening, and she coaches her extended family on how to surf the net.

Her first step would be to look for a market in her own company. If she hears that her company has to teach a new point-of-sale computer system being deployed, this could be the perfect market for her skills.

However, she might not find an opportunity inside her company. She needs to talk to friends and associates (especially "outsiders"), read about different companies starting with competitors, some of whom may have training departments, surf the net, read the local business, metro, and feature news. Some ideas she might come up with could include:

- Going back to school to get her teaching certification.
- Getting a job in a training department of a retail store.
- Starting her own business training people to use the Internet.
- Working for an electronics retailer for whom she could teach classes to customers about how to use computers.

Sometimes marketing isn't about what you can do but what your company or your team can do together. Here is a comment on marketing from John Adams, who left a job as an air traffic controller to build an impressive contract cleaning company with 300 "members" (employees) and annual revenue of $3.5 million. Unlike many companies, where marketing is on the external, he stresses the internal.

I've never been good at marketing myself. What has always worked for me is to sell our company through the hard work and achievements of our team of cleaning specialists, special service specialists, and leaders and staff. Shining the spotlight on others reflects back to your strengths as a helmsman.

Always remember that marketing is an internal as well as an external affair. It is of utmost importance to keep your company members informed and aware of your mission and purpose as well as what you offer them in line with product (fulfillment and satisfaction), price (compensation), promotion (corporate hugs) and placement (the work environment).

—John A. Adams, author, *Miracles at Work: Building Your Business from the Soul Up,* Enfield, Connecticut

Whether you are looking for a new job or new business opportunity the principle is the same—opposites attract.

6

GETTING OUTSIDE OF YOUR OUTSIDER SELF

In this chapter we are going to look at techniques for successful networking as an outsider. You will learn how you can meet new people by stressing your unique qualities so that you find new career opportunities. In this chapter you will also find out how to pitch yourself and present your differences in a positive light. Pitching yourself is a vital part of networking and can be the difference between building contacts, which don't lead to jobs, and building relationships, which do lead to opportunities.

> *A little league basketball coach gets a job interview at one of his dream firms because it turns out he is coaching the son of a top executive there.*
> —Caroline Ceniza-Levine, cofounder of SixFigure-Start,__*www.theglasshammer.com/news/2009/04/01/ask-a-recruiter-networking-success-stories/*

Outsider Networking

Many books have been written about networking, but none about how an outsider networks. For many of us who feel different it can be a daunting, and even impossible task. We don't feel part of a group so how do we jump into a group and start networking? Many of us assume that because we can feel outside of society, we can't be part of it.

It is a dull but true fact that being an outsider is about letting people know who you are. We get scared of this. We think that we will never meet the right person. We think that we will fail. We hide in front of the TV.

> *It isn't just what you know, and it isn't just who you know. It's actually who you know, who knows you, and what you do for a living.*
> —Bob Burg, author, *Go Givers Sell More*, Portfolio Hardcover, 2007

Everyone Is Making It Up

No one has all the answers (not even me). Our society gives the impression that some people know and other people don't. It's really not true. Every time you find an "expert" who has the definitive answer, another pops up who has another view. Even if you get most of the experts to agree, you will still find someone who breaks the rules successfully.

We outsiders believe that some people must know more than we do. Instead of feeling comfortable talking to someone on the bus or at a breakfast joint we feel uncomfortable. We make their expensive suit, or their education, or experience some reason to feel inferior.

So where does that leave you with networking? That it's a lot easier than we think, because there are many ways to be successful—none of which are the only way. Of course we can learn from experts and some of their advice may be very good and work for us. We can also reject their advice and go to other experts or non-experts. Finally, we can make it up ourselves.

It's All a Game

Most of us take networking very seriously, but I have been most successful when I have made networking a game. You can decide what the game is, and it can motivate you to do better. You can make the game meeting as many people as possible, staying for 40 minutes whether the event is good or bad, or trying to find the one person who knows about a particular company. Whatever the game is, establish your rules, including how you win, and then stick with them. The rules of meeting people might be, you must meet as many people as possible and meeting people means you exchange names and companies and ask at least one question. You win by meeting at least 20 people or beating your previous record. The rules of staying at the event could be that you must be in the room (not the bathroom), you can't be on the phone, and you must talk to people (not hiding in the corner admiring the fire extinguisher). You win by staying for a set period of time or beating a record. The rules for the last game are that you ask people until you find the person who knows the company you are interested, and the game might have many rounds at different events. You win by meeting the person.

If we don't play we can never win. No networking means no network. But how can we be successful in networking? By doing it in a different way. I call my tips the Outsider Networking Notions.

Four Outsider Networking Notions

Most books about career networking will insist that you need to meet new people, that you should go to networking events, that you must be asking for a job, and that you need to get out into the world as much as possible. Most books make it sound as though you should go from a networking breakfast where over coffee and donuts you dish out a dozen or so business cards; onto a job fair where you plaster the room with resumes; and then to a "pink slip" cocktail party where you collect as many phone numbers as humanly possible.

1. Network with people you already know.
2. Network where job hunters don't.
3. Network with people not to get a job.
4. Network on your own.

1. Network with people you already know

Many experts will say that networking is all about meeting new people. Maybe. But that is tough. As outsiders we may be nervous about meeting new people: *What will they think of us? Will they wonder why we are different? What will we say and will we make a fool of ourselves?* Why should you start with people you don't know? Why not start with the people you do know.

Everyone knows someone. (Except the monk on top of the mountain who is probably not looking for a job right now so we won't worry about him at the moment!) We all know people, and they know us. They know we are different and we don't have to explain who we are.

Eighty percent of my business has come through knowing people—not networking. I didn't go out to meet new people; I talked to people I already knew. I went to the United States on a great job because I had made friends with the person running the project. I sold my best-selling book by going to a dinner party and meeting someone. I worked for the BBC in Tokyo because I met someone at a conference. I optioned my first screenplay to someone I met at a brunch. I sold this book through a contact I made through LinkedIn.

I advise my clients to start with people they know. Your family and close friends are more likely to understand and support you than people who don't know the inner you and only see the outer differences. The main tool I use in Notion One is the networking circle.

Networking circle

I look at networking as a circle with a series of levels ranging from One to Four.

Level one

First, at the heart of the model, there is our family and close friends. The people at Level One know us well. They often care deeply about us and will help us willingly. Some of them know us better than we know ourselves. Some of them, many of them maybe, are misfits or outsiders too. We should start networking there. They will be willing to help you, and may surprise you with who they know. My sister was a teacher but has met the Queen of England and the Duke of Edinburgh twice. Not that I expect her to pass on my resume to Elizabeth Windsor (the queen) but you get the point. So engage with the people who don't care about how professional your questions are, or are willing to brainstorm with you. They will come up with new ideas, unique approaches, and ways to show off your differences.

Level two

Close friends and family may not have the contacts you need. They may not work in the industry you're targeting or know the people who would buy your product. So spreading the word through professional targeted contacts is required.

Level Two is your current business and personal contacts. Those could include your current work colleagues, people you know professionally, such as clients or vendors, and people you interact with in professional work groups. On the personal side it can include your friends, neighbors you hang out with, and even relations you don't see on a regular basis but with whom you are currently in touch—meaning the past six to 12 months.

They may be outsiders too or they may understand or be interested in outsiders. They will have an affinity with you. If they don't they probably should not be in Level Two.

These people like you, but do not love you, and will be willing to help. They may not do your laundry the way your mother does but they will be able to help you with the name of a person to call, or a good tip on a possible job opening. Of course they also have their circles of friends so the one person you know in your apartment building may introduce you to two other people who live there, and they may have friends across town, and so it goes.

People in your Level Two probably provide much more information than your close friends and family in Level One simply because there are more of them. The sheer numbers say they have better job intelligence.

Level three

Next are those contacts who are either not current or not as close. In the not-current bucket include your classmates from high school or college; coworkers from previous jobs, or friends and family who have moved away or you lost contact with. With the Internet you can connect with these old contacts fairly easily. There are sites that can reconnect with prior schoolmates, coworkers, friends, and family. These people liked you at one point, and if you reach out the relationship may well be rebuilt in short order. They can help you and, if you approach them in the right way, will be willing to give you information. Obviously, this is an even bigger circle of contacts with even larger coverage and knowledge.

They too may be outsiders or empathetic to being different. The difference is that they are not current contacts or are not as close as some of your other relationships.

Level four

You have identified a number of people you want to know. They include potential employers or customers as well as mentors or experts. How do you get to these people? You don't know them, right? Right! But your contacts in Levels One through Three may, and often do. Researching them so that you have information on where there may be common bonds is a good start. Knowing that a potential employer is involved with the Red Cross means that you could ask your contacts for links to that charity and then to the possible new boss.

Use your networking circle to meet those people you don't know through the people you do. But also be clear that you want to meet people in this level who are sympathetic to you and your perspective on life or your outer differences. Seek out those people who intrigue you, or with whom you have affinity, or who seem to have outsider qualities themselves.

2. Network where job hunters don't

Career books advise job hunters to go to job fairs, breakfasts for job seekers, and mixers for people in your industry. The problem with that advice is that there are a lot of people all wanting the same thing—a job. Many job fairs, especially in a down economy, will have far more applicants than jobs. You will be competing against all kinds of people, some who will have equal or better qualifications.

The problem with these kinds of events is that you will be an outsider among a lot of insiders. As an outsider you may have to work even harder than other attendees at these events. If you are older, or have a disability, or are just a little eccentric, many employers will make a judgment based on first impressions and spend time with someone who fits their profile better. This is definitely prejudice but it does happen.

Where do you network? As outsiders, you are used to thinking out of the box, doing things differently, and taking advantage of a unique worldview. Take that ability and apply it to networking.

Why go to a job fair where there are more people looking for jobs than people who can offer them. Why not go to an event where there are far more people who can hire you than people looking.

A smarter approach would be to network at places where other job hunters are not networking. If you want to work in a call center, find out a professional group for call center managers and go to a meeting or join a group online. Call center managers can hire you, so these are the people you want to know.

Or you could spend time with a group of parents who are raising kids through your kid's school or play group. Talk to them about jobs and job opportunities. Most of those parents are probably not looking for jobs but their spouses, family members, and friends will have information about jobs, and will be able to hire you.

If this doesn't work, volunteer or take a class. Doing something or learning about something you are passionate about is a great way to meet people. There will be a few people who are like you looking for a job, but there will be far more who are in a position to offer you a job or at least give you some information.

3. Network with people not to get a job

One big mistake I see job hunters make is that they believe networking is all about getting a job. Let me explain what I mean. Many people will go to a networking event, introduce themselves, and ask people for any job leads. That normally doesn't work because it's like cold-calling or selling through direct mail: You have to talk to a lot of people before you make a sale, with direct mail the response rate is sometimes only 1 or 2 percent. Asking people you don't know at a networking event for a job will probably produce the same kind of results. If you are an outsider, then your results may be even worse.

I always advise clients to use networking as a way of building relationships. Only when someone likes and trusts you is he or she willing to go the extra mile for you. Focus on networking as a way of getting to know people. In every conversation you should always come away with a piece of information or the name of someone you can talk to—not a job lead or offer.

When someone gives you information or another contact you can build a relationship. You find out if the information is useful. You go back to the contact and let them know what you discovered. They learn something and gives you another piece of information. You call them back. Suddenly you have a relationships and maybe even a friendship. The same applies to contacts.

Outsiders have a unique advantage over insiders: They are different, so they know different friends. An insider may only know the people inside the group. That means that they don't know the outliers. The outliers are those people who are outside of the normal trends. They are often creating the next trend or inventing new possibilities.

4. Network on your own

The Internet is also a powerful way of spreading a form of "electronic word of mouth." Blogs, newsletters, and well-visited Websites can carry your marketing messages to large worldwide audiences. These messages can lead to job opportunities, freelance contracts, and customers, especially from Level Four.

As an outsider you can do different things to make a splash. Many U.S. universities are asking for video applications, which applicants send in as DVDs or load onto a Website such as YouTube. The admissions teams are looking for grades and scores but also something that they almost can't define—a unique quality, which tells them that the person will add greatly to the student body or go on to do great things in the future. This can be seen in the Internet video of "Math-Girl Ballet Dancer," a woman who is a self-identified geek and loves to dance. Her video had 10,000 hits. That means a potential network of thousands of people whom she has never met and has not even talked to.

However, you may know that a company is hiring and you simply want to know more about that company. You can use the search feature through Facebook, LinkedIn, Plaxo, or one of the other social networking sites to learn as much about a company as possible. You can look at the company's page and see what it says and see what others are saying.

You can also be creative and look for competitors. You can search the names of the officers of the company and see what they are interested in outside of work. As an outsider you may find other outsiders. You can also start with what you are interested in and then link to the companies or organizations you are interested in.

But there is also another feature that you can use to find out more about a company in your job hunt. You can use the "find past coworkers" search option to search for individuals who have worked for the company. You can receive quite a different perspective from individuals who no longer work there. Yes, some may not have liked the job, but others will be honest about the type of work being done. If you feel comfortable doing so for the sake of your career change, you can ask these individuals what they thought of the company.

As you network, you have to promote yourself, and that leads us to pitching.

Pitching

Outsiders are often reluctant to share who they are. In the past when they did reveal information about themselves it may have gone badly with people. People may have questioned them, teased or ridiculed them, or even rejected them because of what they presented.

Pitching is listening

But I am here to say that pitching yourself doesn't need to be difficult, hard, and painful. We make it scary because we buy in to the stereotypes of pitching—hard selling, cold calling, knocking down doors.

Even these very phrases make it sound tough. Most people are not natural salespeople, and they get overwhelmed and confused by the slick, smooth, successful sales guys and gals pitching their hearts out, whom they see in movies or being interviewed on TV or performing on the Home Shopping Network or QVC. These professionals make it look so easy.

The funny thing is that it is easy. Not when we think of it as sales, but when we think of it as communication. And communication starts with listening, which is not only what is said—that only accounts for 7 percent of the message but with how it is said—the tone and pitch which makes up 38 percent of the message, and what is not said or the non-verbal communication which is the remaining 55 percent. When we take notice of the person who is listening we can start to communicate rather than pitch. Most good salespeople don't see pitching as a one-way presentation they see it as two-way communication. They have a careful message but how they deliver it and what they don't say is based on what they see in their audience.

Many outsiders are very good at reading audiences because they have in the past had to be on their guard. They have looked out for when the person listening is not paying attention or is agitated or is getting angry. These are great skills to have in pitching because you can take the standard message you are going to deliver and flex, fix, and flourish it to make it work.

There is no perfect pitch divorced from an audience. There is only a perfect pitch for a specific person or people. This relieves the pressure. You don't have to do the pitch in a certain way, which may feel foreign to you. You have lots of options about how you pitch as long as you are connecting with the receiver of your information. So now that we have seen how pitching is about the audience, let's look at the basics of the pitch message.

When you are talking to someone you need to be able to explain who you are, what you do, and what you want, in a brief, interesting and compelling way.

How to pitch? PUN.

So how do we pitch ourselves?

Let's start with thinking about a pitch as if it was a headline in an article, the trailer for a film, or the subject line of an e-mail. What is it that pulls you in, makes you want to read more, or in the case of the movie buy a ticket and see it? It's three things—PUN—no *pun* intended.

P: personal connection. Your pitch needs to connect with the person you are talking to. It has to have some relevance to resonant with your target, the more relevance, on more levels, the more impact it carries. As an outsider you need to either find other outsiders or insiders who value outsiders and can see the power and impact of your outsider qualities.

U: useful information. Your pitch must include something that the target wants or needs. The target should be thinking, "Wow, that's going to solve a problem we've been facing" or "Of course, that's exactly what I need." As an outsider you need to know enough of the insider world to be able to determine what will work and what won't work. Something that is too expensive, takes too long, or is too challenging for the culture will be seen as not useful and will be rejected.

N: ideally it includes something new. If it is something that the targets have direct interest in and finds useful then they may take action but you need to have that extra to make them buy. The information has to be useful and new. It has to be different from what they have heard. If it's new—either brand-new or a new spin on something old, they are more likely to focus and follow through.

If recruiters have heard the same pitch from the last ten job hunters they will be happy to hear something useful and new. Clients will feel the same if they always hear the same old tired solutions to their problems and suddenly an outsider comes in with something new.

Elevator pitches (you don't really have to be in an elevator!)

Many career books talk about the "elevator speech": the 30-second version you have ready to persuade a future boss you encounter in a Macy's elevator to give you a job, or at least a further opportunity to discuss it. It could also be the short pitch you make to someone at a party about your new business or the freelance work you want to secure.

Let's see an example of PUN in action for one of these elevator speeches or passing conversations you may have when networking.

PUN example

You're a project manager with tons of experience implementing new computer systems. But although you're good at the technical side of your job, you're also a bit of an outsider in your current company because you are always thinking about the end user. Your boss's view is that training is when you need to think about the person using the new system. You disagree, and believe that the focus on the human side has to be built in from the beginning. So, here's the scenario.

Auntie Regina's ribs

You're at a barbecue at your aunt's house and she introduces you to a guy she's known from high school who is something big in technology. Well that's how she introduces him. Okay, roll tape, lights, and action—you're on for your pitch.

So first of all, relax. This is a barbecue. The guy has ketchup on his shirt. He's smiling. Have some fun and remember PUN.

You: "Hi, how's it going?"

Guy with ketchup: "Good, your aunt sure knows how to grill steaks."

You: "Yep, she's the best."

Guy with ketchup: "What do you do?"

You: "I'm a project manager with MicroMaxo Systems."

Guy with ketchup: "You are? I worked for them back in the 1980s."

SCORE 1—You have made a Personal connection.

Guy with ketchup: "Really. I'm working on a couple of systems for a bank. That's what my company specializes in. I partnered with a woman from "National Bank, Amiar Trent, and we run the company together. We're really busy right now—can barely keep up with the work. And it's always tough finding good people.

SCORE 2—You have made an impact on the Useful side. He's busy. He needs people. You may be the kind of "people" he needs.

You: "I'd be interested in talking to you more. I'm a project manager who not only meets all the deadlines and keeps under budget, but really thinks about the end user. That's my passion—the human side of systems."

Guy with ketchup: "Great. You know why it's hard to find the right kind of people? It's because most project managers don't think of the end user and then we end up having to go back and rewrite half the code. It's great to hear a different story. Let me get another beer and we should talk some more."

SCORE 3—N for new. The guy with the ketchup on his shirt has heard a different view and he likes it. The pitch worked.

The Long and the Short of It

So what comes next? We looked at the short pitch, so now we can start looking at longer pitches. A pitch can be delivered in a few sentences or the pitch can be much longer and woven into the course of a short conversation. The length of the pitch will depend on how much time you have available, how complex your message is, and how receptive the receiver is to your pitch. Whether you are taking 30 seconds or 30 minutes, PUN will still be an effective way to structure the exchange.

As you know PUN is like a headline, trailer, or subject line on an e-mail. Now we can talk about the article, the movie, or the e-mail—the longer pitch. You've hooked the person, but now you have to compel him or her to action. Rather than a list of projects you've worked on, companies you've worked for, or people you know, a story is the most succinct way to communicate your value proposition in a way that is both effective and memorable.

Tell Your Story

As we know from childhood, every story must have a beginning, middle, and end. There had to be set up and a pay off. We instinctively know when a story is not working, and yet many of us find problems with creating stories. Stories exemplify our uniqueness. They help employers to hire us, clients to take on our services, and customers to buy our products.

Let's see PUN in action in a longer version.

Auntie Regina's ribs—more sauce

Here's an example. We'll go back to the barbecue. Guy with ketchup on shirt is listening to your story.

Guy with ketchup: "So tell me more about what you've been up to."

You: "Last year I was working on a new system for a client, International Bank. I had met with the people at the bank and discussed our plan. The system was going to help bank tellers increase accuracy and save time per transaction. I asked if my team could talk to some tellers to get their input. The client said, no, we didn't need to, and that she knew all about the teller role and would answer any questions for us."

Let's Start at the Very Beginning

Let's stop here. That was the beginning of the story. We've given the set-up. We've explained what the current status was. We've talked about what we inherited and we're ready to start talking about what we did—the middle of the story. Too often, that's where people start so that the target doesn't know the context or why the actions were important. Now, we can move on to the middle of the story.

The middle comes next

You: "I wasn't really happy with that answer. I knew from experience that if you didn't get the end users' input early you could have big problems. And I also knew that my client was going to be too busy to give me the time I needed and might well not have the hands-on information I needed. But she was the client."

Guy with ketchup: "Tough call."

You: "Yes, but I knew what to do. I pulled some examples, case studies that showed why having the end-users' input was so important. When I showed them to her she understood and gave me the names of some of her top people."

So that's the middle of the story. You might want to add more to your own story, but like any good joke it's really the setup and the pay off that get the biggest laughs. And now to end up how about the end of the story?

All good things have to end

Guy with ketchup: "Good work. I bet having some good examples helped your case."

You: "Yes. And when the system went live we had no problems. The users really liked it and the upgrade from their old process was really smooth. The manager told me that she was really pleased I had pushed her to get feedback from the users, and that had made all the difference."

Guy with ketchup: "Fantastic."

There you go. That was an example of a story, or a longer pitch that would get you an interview. Or if you were running a business or consulting, it would get you the meeting and specs to do a proposal.

Here's another fabulous real-life example from Ron Shimony that shows the importance of believing in yourself. This is his initial experience with pitching himself.

> *I walked up and down Lincoln Avenue in the north suburbs of Chicago and started applying for sales jobs at various car dealerships: "Hi, my name is Ron Shimony, and I would like to work for you. I don't have any car sales experience, but I can learn fast" was what I would tell the manager. And "No thank you, we don't have any openings right now," or "Sorry, we don't hire people with no sales experience," were the two most common answers I received.*

And then he saw where he was going wrong.

> *I realized that I had been asking these sales managers for the right to apply for a job with their company, instead of expecting them to hire me. I had to show the value I would bring to the table, billing myself as the best potential car salesperson these managers ever met.*

Along with this belief in himself, Ron also practiced his pitch and emphasized his positive qualities through his body language and delivery. This was his new pitch.

Hi, my name is Ron Shimony, and I would like to work for you. Although I do not have any car sales experience, I can assure you that no one can outwork me. I will become your number-one sales guy, if you just give me the opportunity! I know what I can do and achieve, and you will not be disappointed" was my modified introduction. *"I am a fast learner, and your company will benefit greatly from my selling abilities and enthusiasm.*

Not surprisingly, a Chicago dealer hired him.

"You're hired! Are you ready to start tomorrow morning?"
"Why wait until tomorrow when today is still here?" I replied.
"I like you already, Ron,"
—Ron Shimony, Speaker and Author, Schaumberg, Illinois

7

TOOLS TO SELL YOURSELF

Information about job hunting abounds in books, magazines, newspapers, Websites, and through courses and seminars. This book is about how an outsider goes through the job search process. Having coached everyone from factory operators who have not completed high school, to CEOs of major corporations with more schooling than anyone could imagine, I find conventional job-hunting advice flawed. Most experts are focused on the traditional process of getting a job: write the perfect resume, attach the even more perfect cover letter, send to relevant job postings on a job site, wait for the recruiter to call you for an interview and offer you the new position. That may work for some people, but the majority (80 percent according to some research) don't find their jobs that way! In the last five years, I worked with a senior executive who found a job paying nearly $500,000 and a payroll clerk earning about $50,000. Both had been laid off and both got their new jobs through routes that most career advice books don't even mention or would discount!

In this chapter, we'll look at the tools that really work to help you sell yourself and get to that crucial job interview.

Presenting Yourself

What are some of the tools that you will need to present or sell yourself and get the job or the consulting work? There are two types of tools for outsiders to promote themselves.

First, we'll discuss the tools that you can use to *present yourself* including effective ways of working with a resume and a cover letter, and the use of other online tools such as an online profile, blog, or personal Website.

Second, we'll look at the outlets you can use for *finding a job* or a consulting contract, such as Monster.com (general job site) or TheLadders.com ($100,000 + jobs) or elance.com (freelance work) and examine which ones work and which ones don't. Let's start out with the tools to present or sell yourself.

Presenting Yourself—Resumes

Here's something lots of career experts won't say: A great resume doesn't guarantee you a job, great or otherwise. So why bother?

The resume, the actual piece of paper, is usually not what gets you the job interview. The networking gets you the interview. I sometimes joke that you could write, "I am a good salesperson and I want to make $100k" on a napkin as your resume and cover letter combined, and you could get a job if you had the right contacts.

When I went to leave the company a few years later, the head of the department was on medical leave for cancer. He called his boss and told him to offer me any management job they could to get me to stay. He said they were losing too much talent.
—Donna Schilder, PCC, Leadership & Career Coach
Glacier Point Solutions, Inc.

So why spend all that time on a resume? I believe some people like to work on resumes because they are safe. They sit at home and create perfect sentences and avoid making calls and going out to meet people. By crafting their resumes, they can say that they were busy working on their job hunt and they don't have to feel guilty. That's the wrong reason.

The right reason is to focus on where you want to go in your career and what you have achieved. The thought process behind a great resume is vital. Working out how to present your strengths (and address any deal-breaking weaknesses) in one or two pages (or three if you are superstar with lots of experience) is a valuable exercise that enables you to speak more effectively about who you are and why someone should hire you. For an outsider this process (not the result) is vital. You want to make sure you present your differences in a way that are a turn-on rather than a turn-off to an employer.

Resumes are pitches

A resume is another kind of pitch. Just as a verbal pitch is like the trailer for a movie, or the headline of a news article, or the subject line of an e-mail, so too is a written pitch—or resume. The trailer gets a person into the movie theater. The headline gets someone to read the entire story. The subject line gets the reader to open the e-mail. And the resume gets the prospective employee into the interview.

As an outsider, you are more like an independent movie than a Hollywood Blockbuster, or a local newspaper with a different edge rather than a national edition, or a quirky and personal e-mail from a friend who makes you stop and open it rather than a highly produced and stylish update on your credit card.

A selling tool

Resumes should be complete and accurate, but they are also selling tools. They should not be fictional, but should present you in the best possible light. A resume is a way to attract people to you. How well you know the employer dictates how much the resume must sell you. As an outsider you may have already experienced rejection because you are different. You want to make sure you limit the reasons a recruiter will say no and increase the reasons to say yes.

When an employer reads a resume he or she should be attracted enough to call you in for an interview. The interview is like the news article. It should be interesting, informative, and answer all questions the employer has about you, the prospective employee.

Balancing Who You Are With What They Want!

Employers want three things: someone who can do the job, someone who will fit in, and someone who won't cause trouble! As an outsider you may have issues on all three fronts, but especially on the second and third issue. If you have spent time traveling around the world, some recruiters will see that as a red flag that you are going to cause trouble. By that I mean that you will stay for six months and then decide to go off diving in the Red Sea and never come back. So as you write your resume you need to equate what makes you different with what the employer wants in this job. If the recruiter wants someone who has travel experience so that he or she can relate to the customers in his store who are all world travelers themselves, then play your experiences up. If he wants someone who has never left the state don't mention that your passport is full up with stamps from around the world.

Short and Sweet

Covering the past 10 years is usually enough information. Experience beyond that is usually dated, less relevant, and can also enable ageist employers to reject you. Pick out the key elements that highlight what makes you different from your peers. The danger is that we want to include everything.

We put so many of our fabulous and not-so fabulous achievements in our resumes that we dilute our valuable message points with clutter. We talk about our fabulous achievements designing revolutionary products that have won a number of international awards, and that we are also members of the Holiday Party Planning Committee. It's nice that we helped with the festival occasions in the office, but most employers really don't care. So unless you are applying for job requiring event-planning skills, this information doesn't need to be included in your resume.

Format Counts

The format of the resume is just as important. Although you may be unique and special, I have found that resumes that are unique and special tend to get ignored. So avoid fancy stuff. Complicated fonts and elaborate graphics discourage the reader from continuing. Too many CAPITALS and **bold** and <u>underlines</u> can make the work look untidy and disorganized. Fonts that are bigger than 12 point makes the resume seem overstated, if not childish. On the other hand, too small a font— below 10 is my rule—makes the text illegible. The average reader takes 20 to 30 seconds to read a resume so if recruiters are straining to read the font, they will simply give up before they even start. Changing the color of the font is also a no-no. Symbols, even happy ones like this ☺ are irritating and either neutralize the effect of the message ☺ or annoy the reader ☹. They tend to blow up 💣 and should be avoided. The time to have fun as a successful outsider is not with the resume, but with your pitch, interview, or presentation.

DAVID COUPER
ADDRESS, L.A., CA ZIP
PHONE, info@davidcoupercoach.com

Career summary

A coach and training professional with fifteen years' experience coaching individuals and developing strategic training and organizational development solutions for Fortune 500 companies. He has designed for online and classroom training and for blended solutions. His expertise includes coaching, leadership, team-building, change management, diversity, culture shifts, conflict resolution, recruiting, succession planning, and performance management. He is a dual U.S./UK citizen.

Professional experience

Transitions Coaching/DAC Associates—Los Angeles, Calif.
Director—July 2007 to present
Principal of Consultancy Company. Selected accomplishments include:

- Designed workshop materials for up-selling. (Clarity—Valley Crest)
- Developed corporate university for sales associates and store managers including selling skills and product knowledge. (Barbecues Galore)

Countrywide Home Loans—Pasadena, Calif.—July 2006 to July 2007
Vice President—Training and Development

- Responsible for three reports. Position reports to 1st Vice President Training.
- Created new group responsible for analyzing and planning training solutions working with senior management on prioritizing and sourcing resources.
- Managed development of change management for three major system rollouts.
- Managed redesign of classroom training for blended approach.

- Developed training solutions for compliance issues, legislative updates, HR performance appraisal process, customer service, and sales performance issues.

DAC Associates—Los Angeles, California
Director—Feb. 1997 to July 2006
Principal of consulting company. Selected accomplishments include:

- Managed design and development of leadership training programs for supervisors and managers. (Miller Brewing, Golden State Foods, Marin Journal, Mattel)
- Led change management project as the result of a merger between two departments, which resulted in a significant cultural shift. (Ameritech)
- Developed performance development program. Program rated 4.8 (5 scale) and produced a significant improvement in customer service. (Bright Medical)
- Created OD and training strategy with senior team: conducting a training needs analysis; developing a 5-year implementation plan. (Kaiser Permanente)
- Coached senior executives on career development and job transition (manager to SVPs). (Fox, Sony, E! Entertainment, St. Joseph's Health Care, Bosch)
- Developed and designed cultural strategy and delivered culture-shock training for senior executives on global assignments. (The Gap, Arco, Nestle)

Arthur Andersen—Chicago, Illinois
Manager—Feb. 1993 to Feb. 1997

- Invited to the U.S. to work as part of internal training division developing solutions for tax, accounting, and consulting professionals (90%). Also assigned to client projects (10%).
- Led 5-member client team as part of Bell South $40M change management and re-engineering project. Worked with executive team to design learning strategy.

- Designed and developed quality improvement program for Tax Practice.
- Researched and developed change integration process for experienced hires for all divisions including mentoring, buddy-system, and change education. Turned around retention problem and demonstrated ROI on design and development.
- Conducted needs analysis as a result of Andersen's merger with Japan's largest accounting firm. Developed HR, training, and acculturation strategy as a result. Research gathering included onsite visits, surveys, and focus groups.
- Managed design of live business television program, shown to 2,500 viewers, on the use of the Internet. Also hosted program on-air. Awarded Best Program Produced by Private Satellite Network in USA (TelCon). Managed 25 people and budget of $1.5M in the development of a 4-day education seminar for 1,000 people. Delivered under budget by 10%. Seminar was highest ever rated (4.72 on 5 scale) and won a national award.

Education

Santa Monica University—Santa Monica, California, Masters in Psychology, Spiritual Psychology, Communication, Counseling.

Royal Society of Arts—London, UK
Graduate Qualification in Education

University of Wales—Cardiff, UK
BA Honors Communication, Communication theory including psycholinguistics and sociolinguistics.

Training

Development Dimensions Incorporated, Pittsburgh, Pennsylvania
Certified to train trainers in 50 courses on leadership solutions.

Datasolve Education—Manchester, UK
Graduate Diploma in developing computer-based training.

Publications

People Skills—Gower Publications UK/HRD Press USA 1993
Activities for developing interpersonal skills. Translated into four languages.

Role Plays for Developing Counseling Skills—Gower Publications UK 1993
Role plays cover lay-offs, alcoholism, etc.

Presenting Yourself: Cover Letters

You can never know what happens to a cover letter. Some cover letters are electronically scanned, some are read, and some are tossed! You can't afford to take the risk of not doing a cover letter when your future employer may read and analyze each one. It's one of those things that you have to do, like having your vaccination shots as a kid. You just never know when you are going to need them.

But remember to be professional. Even if you are a wacky dude, your letter needs to follow conventional format.

A cover letter can serve any one, or all, of six functions:

1. **Hook the Reader:** Cite personal referrals that will open doors, ways you can solve their current business needs, specific experience that will aid your application, and make sure you highlight why you are special.

2. **Mirror the Job Posting:** If the job asks for Oracle experience, include the word Oracle. But don't make the matching obvious. For example, if the job posting states the candidate must be an excellent team player and you write, "I am an excellent team player" in your cover letter—you've been too blunt. It would be better to say, "I worked in a team of 10 which was recognized as the best sales team two years running."

3. **Highlight Your Relevant Accomplishments:** Make sure you talk about specifics in the cover letter. Often people

will say, "I'm an excellent salesperson." It is much better to write something similar to, "I increased sales by 10 percent, making my division the highest-producing unit in the company."

4. **Give the Employer Extra Information About You:** Use the cover letter to answer the show-stopper question. Some employers reading my resume would see that my first degree was from the UK and begin to think and worry about visas and legal immigration status. This could easily have been an issue that would prevent the employer from calling me in for an interview. So, I added "dual U.S./UK citizenship" to my resume, and for good measure elaborated further in the cover letter, "I am a dual U.S./UK citizen who has worked in the Midwest and California for more than 15 years. I am also able to work legally in the countries of the European Community, including my home country Great Britain."

5. **Add the Juicy Personal Info You Can't Include in a Resume:** This is where you can showcase your Outsider talents that don't easily fit into the resume. For example, Petco, the well-known retailer who caters to your dogs, cats, and other animals, values you owning a pet. Your personal pet situation does not fit well in a resume, but goes great in a cover letter! So you might write, "I would love the opportunity to work for Petco since my Labrador, Harry, and I have been faithful customers for the last five years. I have always connected well with the friendly and professional staff of fellow pet lovers and would be honored to be part of that team."

6. **Get in and out Real Quick:** I usually recommend a one- or two-line hook and then two or three bullets with accomplishments. Weave these in to the letter with the key words or phrases from the posting that you want to match. And above all, make sure you emphasize why you are different from the competition and how that will benefit the employer.

Having looked at how to present yourself, now let's look at ways of using social networking to promote your brand.

Promoting Yourself: Online Resumes, Blogs, and Personal Websites

Having an online presence makes sense. If you are working, but are interested in other opportunities, the more information you have about yourself out on the Internet, the more employers and customers can find you. If you have skills that are in demand, or are in a job for which there is a shortage of qualified candidates, recruiters may actively be searching for you, and being online makes it easier for them to do so. Perversely as it may seem, if you are working in a good job you will be in greater demand. It's like finding out that a restaurant is all booked up for the next six months—we assume that means it's terrific, and we all want a reservation. Employers assume that if you are in a job you must be good.

If you are working in a job that does not use some or all of your outsider qualities, those qualities you use for your hobbies or outside activities, then an online presence may be a great way to go. We will look at personal online marketing strategies first, and then discuss social networking sites. But before we do, a short discussion on one important rule of online marketing and promotion: Always assume your potential (and current) employers can or will see everything about you that is, or ever was, on the Internet.

Google Search gets more powerful every day. Even after you "delete" Web content about you, it remains "cached" on the Internet, and there are search engines that do nothing but cached content searches. The higher up you go on the career ladder, the more extensive the search your current or prospective employer will conduct. The bigger the company— think Fortune 500—the greater the search, even if the job is entry level. This is also true depending on how sensitive the nature of the job position is; for example, working with or consulting for a defense contractor, or working as a staffer in a State or U.S. Congressman's office.

So that picture of you wearing a silly hat drinking tequila body shots and beers on New Year's Eve at the local pub? Yes, that one. That one your friend put on her Facebook page with your full name in the caption? Busted!

Online resume and portfolio

An online resume is simply a resume that is online. It can be as simple as a resume that you have loaded onto a job site such as Monster. com; CareerBuilder.com; Google Jobs; a basic static Web page; or the resume may be on your own personal Website with a complex series of Web pages which have graphics, animation, video, audio, and links.

Most online resumes that you upload onto a job site are in the same format as your printed resume. The only difference is that some characters in word processing programs such as Microsoft Word are not read correctly, so you may end up with weird and random symbols instead of a bullet or an apostrophe. To avoid that, you can upload a "text" version of your resume without the formatting, or type it directly into the online database. The text-version method works well, saves a lot of retyping, and avoids potentially adding new typos or errors.

More advanced resumes feature rich text online formats, with online editors that present a way of editing rich text within a Web browser. This enables you to format a resume online without using complicated HTML commands. This can offer your resume interesting style choices, and it is a good idea to use them if you can so your resume doesn't fade into the background.

In an online resume you could include the logos of all the companies you have worked for to make your experience stand out. You could show how your efforts increased profits or sales with an animated graph. You could create and upload a video of you explaining your business philosophy, or give tips for how to plan a successful personal event such as the family reunion you organized. You could record and upload an audio of you being interviewed on blog radio. You could link to any other places where you are being quoted favorably or are contributing positively. There are no rules.

Personal Website

A personal Website can also serve as a resume, but if so, that should be its guiding purpose. It can show off your skills and link to what other people are saying about you. The personal Website should reflect who you are and support your job application. If your Website only talks about Barbie, beer, or bears, that's fine, but unless that is part of your unique proposition it will be off-putting to a recruiter or employer. Don't be tempted to add a couple of pages about your career when the Website's main purpose is about your magnificent obsession whatever that is! Whether or not to link to your personal Website from your online resume elsewhere depends on how tastefully and professionally presented the Website is. Your photo essay of your summer spent building a healthcare clinic in sub-Saharan Africa will play differently than will a photo essay of you drinking 160 different brands of beer over the past five years—unless you are applying for a sales position with a beer company!

Personal blog

A blog—where you comment regularly on matters that interest you, and which reflect your personal outsider view—could be an excellent marketing tool. If your material is well-written, interesting, and useful, you may build traffic and increase your visibility. Be sure that if you start a new blog, it is in alignment with your job and career goals. If you blog about how you want to quit your job and move to Bali, it will not enhance your reputation as a responsible citizen who will be a model employee. Of course if you have a blog, old or new, that is controversial, beware that it may cause problems in your job applications that you may never even know about. Keep in mind that "controversial" is a relative term. Your pro-environment blog may be popular in many circles but might not play well with cosmetics companies, department stores, food companies, and many others that are hyper-sensitive after having dealt with lawsuits and protests from pro-environment groups that these companies truly believe to be unfair or misguided. You will need to explain any possible contradictions between your online and real life persona, if they arise.

Presenting Yourself: Social Networking

Social networking has taken the world by storm. Individuals use social networking Websites to stay connected to their friends and to promote bands, businesses, and more. You can also use it to promote yourself and to gain attention in your career search.

Social networking Websites are also becoming the place to find a job. Companies are utilizing these sites to access some of the most qualified candidates in the world. They're able to do this because there are millions of individuals on these Websites. This means many thousands of them come from specific geographic areas. This is a head hunter's dream.

Twitter enables you to send short messages instantly. You can update someone (tweet) on what you just ate in a new restaurant, the score at the ball game, or the latest news on your industry. You can also use it to connect to people and find work.

When Renee Libby was laid off, she started tweeting. And two months later she had a new job.
—Jessica Dickler, CNNMoney, *http://money.cnn.com/2009/09/03/ news/economy/hired_twitter/index.htm*

Companies create pages on Facebook to promote their product, and they also discuss whether they are hiring. If so, they provide the information necessary to apply.

Facebook enables companies to list advertisements. When you are on your home page, you can look to the right side of the page and most likely see ads. Sometimes these ads are for a product and other times they are for a business. Some ads may state the company is hiring. If that's the case, simply click that ad and you will receive more information on the position and other relevant details. These job ads are targeted to you based on what your profile lists as your current occupation.

Blasting your friends on Facebook can pay off.

Brian Ward lost his job on a Friday afternoon. Eleven days later he had a new one. With nearly 1 in 10 people out of work and the typical job search lasting 12 weeks, how did the Cleveland-based software architect pull it off? In a phrase: online social networking.
—Barbara Kiviat, "Using twitter and facebook to find a job." *www.time.com/time/business/article/0,8599,1903083,00.html*

LinkedIn is a popular social networking site for business. You can create your own profile and expand upon the network of people you know. Add individuals you have worked with in the past to broaden your profile's reach. Make your profile look good—by highlighting your skills and outsider talents—and you will have recruiters contacting you. For example: Project Manager with 10 years of change management experience who has dual U.S./UK citizenship enabling him to work without visa requirements on projects in both the European Community and the USA.

Christine Midwood, a talented technology program director and product manager saw a dramatic difference in how many phone interviews or offers she got from traditional online boards (5% response rate) versus online and offline networking (31% response rate).
—Kathy Robinson, author, "Why LinkedIn is High Octane Fuel for Job Search" *http://blog.linkedin.com/2009/08/11/kathy-robinson-why-linked-in-is-high-octane-fuel-for-job-searching*

Plaxo is another business social networking Website that serves primarily as an online address book that keeps all your contact information as current as possible. Members use Plaxo to store contact information, and that information can be widely accessed so that everyone can stay in touch with each other. Any time an individual changes his or her contact information—a phone number, an e-mail address—the changes automatically appear in the address books of everyone with that individual in their list.

If you use e-mail programs such as Outlook, Mac OS X's address book, or Mozilla Firebird you can also integrate them into Plaxo. It's another way of presenting your information to prospective employers or customers. When you are looking to make a career change, be sure to keep your information as organized as possible. Plaxo consolidates that information keeps it current.

We've looked at various ways of presenting yourself through resumes, cover letters, and online profiles and venues. Now let's look at some of the tools, both online and offline, to help you find a job.

Tools for Finding a Job—Job Sites

Online job searches are now the most commonly used strategy to obtain information and search for potential employers across the globe. Many career experts believe that job sites such as Monster.com or CareerBuilder.com are the keys to success in a job search. Most of these sites offer great advice and tips, list lots of jobs, and can help you in the job search process. But they are only one tool, and a blunt one at that. Networking is still a vital part of your search and a more targeted and more effective one. As an outsider, you have a far better chance at making the case for your uniqueness with a face-to-face contact than going up against a horde of insiders who have applied through a Website.

Getting a job through online search involves several approaches. One is to post your resume on the particular job sites. This covers the companies and institutions that happen to use or search those Websites. When an employer has a job he or she can search the database. Obviously, it is advisable that you post a resume that is structured to meet the needs of the organization for which you want to work, and to fit the activities and duties of the job you seek, so that you appear in that company's search results as often as possible.

This is important because you might miss an ad for a great job, but the odds are good that the employer could find your resume and approach you about the job anyway. It also increases your odds of getting a job because you are not only applying to the jobs that you actually want, but thousands of other employers out there can find your resume and offer you an interview as well if they like what they read. By stressing your differences and how they would benefit a company you will be more likely to get that call.

You can also use these Websites to search for a job. By choosing your field of expertise, job preference, and location you can target opportunities. The Website filters all the data you have given and selects jobs that are closely linked to your field. This can be quite efficient because the Websites have developed software that automatically forwards you all job opportunities close to your preference, daily or weekly, and gives you descriptions and details of how to apply. It is important to keep on updating your profile and resume not only so you can keep up with changing needs, but also so that the new versions get noticed by employers searching.

Many of the Websites will even offer you free e-mail alerts, so that you can be notified each time a new job opening comes up matching your criteria. It can be hard to stay on top of more than one career site, so if you don't want to miss anything, taking a few minutes to set up e-mail updates and alerts are where it's at.

Another advantage of online job sites is that you can apply to many different positions easily and quickly. I advise coaching clients to apply for potentially suitable jobs even if they do not fit all the requirements. For one thing, employers may ask for a candidate that just doesn't exist, or that can't be had at the salary they want to pay, so there is not much but a minute or two to be lost by submitting an application that may miss the mark but might also lead to success. For example, just because an ad asks for a person who is fluent in Spanish and Italian, doesn't mean the employer will hire only the person who meets that requirement. In Southern California it's easy to find someone with Spanish but not with Italian, and the employer may well go with a great outsider candidate even without the language of love!

But a few words of warning. Anyone can pay a fee and list a job posting online. You don't know for sure whether the job even exists. Companies may post jobs on a regular basis even if they don't have one just because they have a contract that requires them to post regularly. Organizations may have a policy that requires advertising a position, but may have already decided on an internal candidate. They go through the motions so that if anyone comes back and says *why did you pick the internal candidate* they can point to the piles of resumes they received from the online posting. Some companies will post a job as a way of researching who's available and what kind of money they make. I am always suspicious of job listings that say, "Must include salary requirements." Maybe I'm old-fashioned but I thought that a company was supposed to set a salary range before they posted a job, and that regard-less of what you were making they would pay the market rate. Yep, maybe I am old-fashioned!

Wait until someone asks you for your salary needs during an inter-view and then give them a range. If you are comfortable sharing that information go ahead, but be aware that the best time to talk about mon-ey is when the employer wants you. That is your strongest negotiating position.

Another variation favored by some less than scrupulous companies is to offer a "job" that pays "up to $100,000 first year" which is actually a franchise or Multi Level Marketing opportunity. If the advertisement seems to be too good to be true, and the employer seems too eager to get you into an interview at a hotel by the airport rather than at their office (often a clue that something is shady), be careful. Don't waste your time on an "interview" that actually turns out to be a sales pitch!

Let's look at how social networking can help you avoid scams and, more importantly, find a great job.

Tools for Finding a Job—Social Networking Sites

You can use the most popular social networking sites such as MySpace, LinkedIn, Plaxo, and Facebook to research a prospective em-ployer or company even if you have no idea whether or not that com-pany has a profile posted on these sites. With more and more companies making themselves available through social networking, you are bound to find a social networking site that will provide you with more informa-tion about almost any target.

When you do additional research on a company outside of its own Website, you can get a multifaceted perspective and gain a sense of security about the company. You can also get an idea of what others think of the company by checking out the profiles of current and former employees who are on the company's friend's lists.

Tools for Finding a Job—Media

How about newspapers, magazines, or professional journals? Although print-based ads still exist, they have rapidly been replaced by online job postings. Smaller companies may use newspaper ads for factory jobs, household help, or hospitality industry jobs. Think about it: If the employer is trying to reach people with print media they are targeting those who may not have computers because they are lower income, or are not computer literate such as some seniors. Trying to reach a more diverse group of people may be another reason to not stick with a purely online job campaign. Some companies like "free papers," given out in some cities, which commuters read on the way to work. These can be good especially for administration or financial jobs. But generally, print media is a minor niche source of positions for most job hunters. To complete our list of job hunting tools, let's look at recruiters and headhunters.

Tools for Finding a Job—Recruiters

Recruiters and headhunters are not your fairy godmothers. They are not going to take your resume, make some calls, and get you that perfect job—well, not 99 percent of the time they are not. It's all about economics. Recruiters and headhunters are paid by the employer—either a flat fee or a percentage of the starting salary—contingent upon finding and placing a new hire. Unlike earlier times, rarely are recruiters paid regardless of the outcome of the search. In the olden days (the 1990s or earlier), an employer would engage a recruiter to find a mid-level or senior person, work out a plan, and give them time to come up with the ideal candidate. Today, it is much more common that the employer is working with multiple recruiters and may even be using their internal team who is also posting the job on major Websites. There is a lot more pressure because if the recruiter is going to get paid and make their rent, car payment or swimming lessons for the kids they have to get the perfect candidate in to the employer and hired as soon as possible. Those recruiters need to be busy finding the right person. If you are the right person, the recruiter will be your new best friend. If you're not, you probably won't even get an automatically generated e-mail response to your inquiry. The recruiters' business is driven by search engagements, not inventory. They can't make money from you if you don't fit the positions for which they are searching.

Unless they are the kind of headhunter firm that works for, and is paid by, the job hunter. These companies will help you with resumes, sending out mailings, giving you advice, and will help you with contacts. Well, that's what they say they will do. Most of them are, unfortunately, ineffective at best and downright scammers at worst. For a fee of just $5,000 to $10,000 they will do what can do better by yourself or with a coach for about a tenth of that price. These companies will often advertise their services for mid-level or senior managers and prey on their fear about not having contacts or job prospects. Before working with any of these companies, who often call themselves employment consultants, placement firms, or job search agencies, check them out thoroughly and carefully consider your alternatives. When I Googled a couple of companies who promised to help "individuals earning six figures" I found a whole bunch of complaints. The Better Business Bureau keeps a list of these companies who make false claims, but they typically avoid detection but reinventing themselves with new, different business names frequently. Remember, no one can get you a job apart from yourself! If anyone promises to get you a job—unless it's Donald Trump or Oprah—don't believe them. And if they want money for that dubious privilege, just say no!

8

Connecting to the Employer, Client, or Customer

Conventional career advice is, at best, conventional. *Conventional* implies that which is accepted by the majority. So it follows that if "conventional" advice could lead to success, then that majority would be successful—which we know is not the case. Real success can occur when conventional wisdom is turned upside down. In this chapter I will share outsider techniques for acing an interview or making a stunningly winning presentation or creating an effective proposal.

Interviewing

Here's a news flash that may shock you: Most interviewers are not prepared for the interview process! Okay, maybe that doesn't shock you, but how about this? Most interviewers are not prepared, are not good at it, and don't even want to be there. Now, you may ask, how do I know this? I know this because I have been one of those interviewers. I have been on interview panels where no one has read the resume ahead of time, prepared questions, or thought about what they are look-ing for in a candidate. The interviewers wanted to hire a good candidate, and they knew it was important, but they were also very busy with fires and putting them out. When the flames are licking under the door, and you can smell the smoke, you are less likely to be interested in a pleas-ant chat with the interviewee than manning the hoses and putting out the conflagration that is threatening to get completely out of control.

My experience is that many employers have had no training on how to interview effectively, have not prepared, and let the interview wan-der from unrelated point to unrelated point. Many of these interviewers will use a few standard questions from a one-page tri-fold pamphlet HR gave them, which creates the impression that they know what they are doing—but it is an illusion. Most small business owners don't even have the pamphlet, though they are more likely to make up for it with sincerity because they are directly and personally impacted by their hir-ing decision.

For the outsider this is an even bigger problem. The inexperienced and unschooled interviewer will not be able to distinguish between first impressions and true discovery. What I mean by that is that many in-terviewers will make decisions based on what they see as you enter the room or hear as you start a phone screening. They will notice the fact that you are a woman and that the hiring manager's team mem-beres are all men, or that you have an "accent" which is not American, or even that you have a pin saying Green Peace attached to your bag. And instead of filing that impression away under "impressions not to be trusted" they will start to hear your career history, accomplishments, and background through that filter. If you are of color or have a disabil-ity or are just different you need to be aware that you have to get over the neophyte interviewer.

I coach clients to take charge and assume that the employer knows nothing! Don't even assume that the employer has read your resume. Don't assume that the employer has prepared a list of questions that will elicit the competencies needed for the job. Don't assume that the em-ployer knows what he or she wants from the prospective employee. And finally, don't assume that this is the perfect job for you. Be sure that you ask questions so that you can decide if you want to work there.

Ask questions and more questions

Even though you may have researched the job and the company, what the employer will want also depends on his or her personal style. If you ask the employer to define what he or she is looking for, then you can more likely meet that need. Even a standard job such as that of a receptionist can vary greatly from one organization to the next. One company wants the receptionist to help out with other office administrative tasks, billing, scheduling, and travel. Another wants the receptionist to focus on the phones. Yet another company wants the receptionist to make clients happy when they arrive.

Gently but firmly lead the interviewer down the path you want to take. Be sure that the employer knows what you have to offer and how your unique character and skills fit in with what the position requires. Be sure to hit the high points and avoid the low points of your career. In an interview, too often we list our weaknesses, talk about our failures, and explain why we are not the most suitable candidate. Instead, we must focus on meeting the needs of the employer or customer. We need to show why the interviewer needs you and explore whether we want to work for the interviewer. It's like a first date!

Do your homework early

When doing research, always start with the company Website. But don't stop there. Google the company and look at page two and three of the search. Sometimes these lesser pages hold gems for you—gems your competition overlooked: a local piece about what the company is doing in the community; a law suit; a comment on a blog about a new product being launched soon. This can be very helpful. The real trick to finding good information about a company is to talk to people who work there, or sometimes even more revealing, who used to work there.

Use social networking as a data mining tool as we explained in Chapter 7. For example, search for people who work for the company you are targeting, or worked there previously, through LinkedIn. Search for employees using the company and then get connected through people you know. Bingo—you have a direct source for up-to-date information on the company. Remember to look for information to help you get the job and to understand if you want the job!

Dress for success: Yep, it matters

Right or wrong, interviews are often won or lost on first impressions. You will need to decide on an outfit. Your appearance is incredibly important in a job interview and you want to create the right impression. You need to dress appropriately for the position, which usually includes a skirt and blouse for women (pants suits are okay in some industries but not in others), and a suit or a sports coat for men.

As an outsider you want to show your flair without looking like a freak. Sorry to be brutal. It's the picture that the employer is interested in, not the frame. So don't distract with a frame that is over-the-top, dated, or just doesn't look right; focus on the picture—that is, the story you present that persuades the employer to hire you. So if you are a guy, wear a sharp, stylish suit with a conservative tie; don't wear one with Mickey, Minnie, or Mighty Mouse on it. If you are a gal, wear a suit—a pants suit might be fine—with no jewelry apart from simple earrings. Don't wear a brooch saying that you "Love Dallas, Doggies, or Donuts."

Bias and Discrimination Happen

Of course as an outsider, some of your differences may be obvious. It may be a sad fact but a reality that an employer may treat you differently because of your ethnicity, or for being disabled or just not fitting in with the stereotype of the corporate culture. If that is the case, you may have to decide if you even want to work there. But the number one overriding goal—always—is **get the offer**, then decide!

Sometimes that bias can work out for you. I was selected to work in the United States because I was not from the States. The company wanted someone who was different. Large companies actively strive to hire diverse people and that can often help an outsider.

And of course the bias can work against you.

As many of you who are different will know, some employers do discriminate. The smart outsider will show why his or her difference provides a benefit.

Once you have perfected your look, and your answers, have friends or someone in your family perform a mock interview with you. They will be able to evaluate your answers, your mannerisms, your appearance, and your level of speech so you know what to work on and improve.

Let's look at the top 10 interviewing questions. I'll use examples based on Pat.

Pat is an administrative assistant. Unlike her colleagues she has lived abroad, loves foreign cultures, and regularly travels. This sometimes makes her feel like an outsider. Pat is an excellent worker and these differences have never got in the way of doing the job.

1. "Tell me about yourself..."

Although technically not a question, this is often how job interviews will start out. As someone in a career transition, you need to outline the most important past events with regard to education, professional positioning and skills in a few minutes flat. Be bold, be brief, and be honest. The interviewer doesn't want to know everything about you. He or she doesn't care about half the things you have done. All he or she wants to know is:

- Can you do the job: Do you have the skills?
- Will you fit in: Are you going to be productive in this team?
- Will you cause any problems: Are you going to leave after two weeks, sue us, get us sued, or be a pain to work with?

Although a common interview question, "Tell me about yourself," properly translated means *I don't know to what to ask. Maybe I will get lucky with this question, or maybe you can help me.* It's a typical approach, but if you go along with the interviewer it's not the most effective way to win in an interview. You are basically throwing pasta against the wall and seeing if it sticks. The main problem is that you don't know what the interviewer wants and needs. You are just guessing. Read this typical interview which includes what the interviewing is thinking as the innocent job hunter goes ahead answering the most common interview question.

Pat (our candidate) is in some ways an outsider. Pat just sometimes feels a bit out of it when talking to friends at work about the latest ethnic restaurant or the next adventure backpacking in Nepal. Pat wants a job that pays the bills, uses Pat's great admin skills, and, if possible, ties to Pat's love of foreign cultures. This is how the interview goes, and we are lucky enough to hear what the interviewer is thinking.

Interviewer: "Hi Pat, tell me about yourself. I am eager to find out what you're made of."

Pat: "Sure. I graduated from MacKenzie College with an AA in business. After I left college, I went to Europe and learned some Italian. I love to travel. I try and get to a new country every year and really explore the culture. It's my thing."

Interviewer's thoughts: I'd like to go to Europe. But we don't need Italian. We need Spanish. I wonder if she knows Spanish. She didn't say anything about it. And what's all this about travel? She's going to be gone half the time. A bit of an oddball this one.

Pat: "When I came back I went into hair-dressing. I did that for about five years and then because of this skin condition I developed because I was allergic to the chemicals, I gave it up. I loved it and I was always experimenting with new styles I learned on my trips."

Interviewer's thoughts: That's interesting. But I don't know need someone who can do hair. And yikes, what chemicals? That's kind of scary. I need to google that. And trips again!

Pat: "I got a job with Acme as a warehouse person. Then after about two years, because I had taken some computer classes, I was given a job as an assistant in the sales department. I spent about five years and then an opening for the chief saleswoman opened up and I tried it and got it. That was fun. I loved all the international work. I also liked that I had to do a lot of travel arrangements. It was almost like traveling myself!"

Interviewer's thoughts: More travel stuff. We don't do any international business. She's not a good fit. The last travel I did was to go to Detroit and that only took 45 minutes.

We have someone who does all our graphics for us so I don't do many presentations but I could learn. Did I mention I like working with our international customers too."?

Interviewer's thoughts: We need that skill. Not good. Who would do the presentations if she can't?

Pat: "Then I worked for the Chief of Marketing. About a year ago, the assistant to the president retired. She was older than me. So they offered me her job. That was cool. Now the company is moving to Texas and I am looking for my next job. I like travel but not to Texas!"

Interviewer's thoughts: *And this isn't the one. Sorry. You're not what we need. It's lucky I am good at interviewing or we could have made a big mistake with Pat.*

Interviewer: "Great! So we're looking at a number of candidates. HR will get back to you in a couple of weeks. Thanks so much for your time."

Pat didn't get the job and doesn't even know why. Pat is a good candidate and thinks that was a good interview. The outsider tendencies have totally gotten in the way of the interviewer seeing what Pat can do and what an asset Pat would be for the company. On the other side, Pat has also not found out what it would be like working for the new boss. Out of the three criteria—getting a job to pay the bills, being valued for her skills, and tying to her love of travel—only one seems to have been met. Here is a different way of approaching the interview.

Answer that open-ended first question briefly, and then begin your own questions to find out what the employer actually wants from this hire. Focus on what you do, not on what makes you different. Highlight what makes you different only as a way of making the sale—that is, as a way of expanding and differentiating yourself from the competition on the needs of the job.

Interviewer: "Hi Pat, tell me about yourself. I am eager to find out what you're made of."

Pat: "I've got 10 years of experience as an admin with Acme Inc working for the President and the Chief of Marketing."

Interviewer's thoughts: *She seems just what we need.*

Interviewer: "Great! That's impressive."

Pat: "Thanks. So before we get much further I wanted to make sure that I give you the information you need. Can you tell me a bit more about the job? I know that I will be supporting you but I wondered what the day-to-day duties were?"

Interviewer: "Well I don't do much travel. But I do have to do a lot of presentations. And I have people calling me all day. I need someone to be a gatekeeper. That's really something personal to me. I know the other managers don't care about the phones but I do. And then it's pretty standard."

Pat: "I get it. Well, I have prepared presentations for my bosses in the past. I did an advanced PowerPoint course last year and that has really helped me. One of my presentations got my last boss a $5M contract. Well, that's what he told me."

Interviewer's thoughts: *I like Pat. Sounds like the presentations would be great. Pat did sales presentations too.*

Interviewer: "Perfect."

Pat: "I have dealt with heavy phones before. My boss who was also in sales had 100 calls a day, sometimes more. I made sure that he wasn't bothered so he could get on with his work. He had a lot of international clients? How about you?"

Interviewer: "Yes, I do too. I don't travel because we have people around the world on the ground, but I have a lot of international dealings."

Pat: "Great. I have a lot of experience dealing with other nationalities and cultures."

Great job, Pat. And even though she doesn't know it the boss will offer Pat the job. The key to this success (and this is the same job as in the first interview—no tricks or funny business here) is that the outsider has stressed her skills and used the outsider tendencies as a positive differentiator, not as a negative distraction.

2. "What do you consider your most significant accomplishment?"

Don't ramble on about everything and anything you've done, from winning first prize in a science fair to having children. Instead, discuss your hard work and accomplishments that relate to the job—and only to this job. Make a list before the interview of your most significant achievements, narrow it down, and then discuss that in two to three minutes. Remember to use stories to get your point across.

Don't let your love of or passion for something that makes you an outsider distract the employer from what you do to meet the needs of the employer.

Pat: "I love PowerPoint. In fact I am kind of a geek. I am always looking for new ways of doing cool stuff. I sometimes spend hours on the Microsoft site trying out different things. One of my presentations won an award on the user blog that I go to. I was really pleased with myself. I spent a couple of weeks solid on it but it was worth it."

Interviewer's thoughts: And how long will it take Pat to do that PowerPoint I need yesterday for the presentation? That's the reality.

Interviewer: "Very interesting. So if you don't have any more questions we'll leave it at that."

A better way of handling this would be:

Pat: "I love PowerPoint. I am really proud of my abilities. I did all the presentations for my boss and one of them was the reason we got this $1 million contract—well that's what my boss said. She said that it was clear, clever, and catchy. I think what makes me unique is that I am always learning new things and can take both my business and artistic sense and build something really different."

Interviewer's thoughts: Great. Seems just the kind of person we want.

Interviewer: "Great. You seem just the kind of person we want."

3. "Why are you leaving your current position?"

Whatever you do, don't badmouth your previous employer or old coworkers. Instead, focus on the benefits of the experience gained in your last position. As an outsider make sure you don't play into an interviewer's hands by giving him or her a reason to think that your maverick nature is what lost you the job.

Interviewer: "And tell me why you left your previous company."

Pat: "I'm very creative—more than most people—and really I had outgrown what I could do for them. I was bored with the work. That's how it went."

Interviewer's thoughts: I knew Pat wasn't reliable. I could tell by looking at what Pat was wearing. Too arty.

Interviewer: "I see. Thank you. Do you have questions for me?

Interviewer: "And tell me why you left your previous company."

Pat: "I really enjoyed working for my last company and I got some great experience, but after five years and after discussing it with my boss, we saw that I wanted a position where I could use my design skills more. I believe that working for your company would be a great fit for my artistic and business sides."

Interviewer thoughts: She really thought it through. I like Pat.

Interviewer: "Sounds like you put a lot of thought into this. I like you Pat and I want my boss to meet you."

4. "What do you consider your biggest weakness?"

An interview is a sales exercise. Soda manufacturers don't advertise their products as sugar water. No, they talk about the positives: how it makes you feel good and quench your thirst. You should do the same. Here is how that might go.

Interviewer: "Tell me about your weaknesses?"

Pat: "I've been in my role for 10 years now and although I'm not perfect, I don't have weaknesses. If I did I wouldn't have won salesperson of the year three years running, and been selected for the Presidents Prize for customer service."

Interviewer: "What prize? How did you win that?"

The interviewer has moved away from weaknesses. But the interviewer might not be so willing to be distracted.

Interviewer: "But what about your weaknesses? You said you weren't perfect?"

So instead of talking about weaknesses talk about something that you have worked on and is now not an issue. Preferably this is something that happened earlier in your career.

Pat: "One challenge I had when I first started as a manager was putting together budget projections. But now, after getting my MBA, I can do those in my sleep. In fact my projections for my present company saved us making some costly mistakes by investing in new machinery that would have been too small for future growth."

Or talk about an issue that everyone knows is an issue.

Pat: "I used to work with offices in London and Sydney. It was tough to keep track of the times. I put up clocks for the three places so that I could be clear. That worked out well."

5. "How have you handled stressful/frustrating/ difficult situations in the past?"

The interviewer is looking to see if you can deal with petty problems on a daily basis. Make sure you address your common sense, perseverance, and patience in these situations. Have a relevant example you can cite. Use one that either highlights how you used your unique persona to solve the issue or shows how you didn't let your being an outsider get in the way.

Interviewer: "How do you handle stressful situations?"
Pat: "Mostly really well. I'm calm and don't get upset. The only time I do is when someone makes something of my disability. I can do every in my job perfectly but sometimes people treat me with kid gloves and it gets my upset. I don't need them to be making me out to be a special case."
Interviewer's thoughts: *Pat has a disability. I didn't know. Sounds like she can get upset. I don't know whether someone who is emotional like that is a good choice.*
Interviewer: "I see. Thank you."

Interviewer: "How do you handle stressful situations?"
Pat: "I'm calm and don't get upset. If I find that there is a lot going on I prioritize and focus on what needs to be done first. I don't get stressed."
Interviewer's thoughts: *Good answer.*
Interviewer: "Good answer. Thank you."

6. "Our company has to deal with...; how would you handle this?"

Don't come up with a complete solution. Instead talk about the process you would go through to get to the solution. These are often trick questions where the employer knows the answer because it is something they have been through. You are at a disadvantage as you don't know the details of the problem, how the culture works and what options have failed. If you launch into a solution which the employer already rejected you don't look smart! Make sure you come up with some out-of-the-box ideas so that you show your outsider skills.

Interviewer: "So tell me how you would deal with this situation? You put together a presentation and make 20 glossy color copies but on the day of the presentation you find that the name of the client is spelled wrong. What would you do?"

Pat: "I am very persuasive. In fact that what makes me different from other people that I won't take "no" for an answer. So I would call every vendor in town until I could find one. I am really pushy sometimes!"

Interviewer's thoughts: That sounds expensive and I don't know whether I want someone that aggressive working on my team.

Interviewer: "So tell me how you would deal with this situation? You put together a presentation and make 20 glossy color copies but on the day of the presentation you find that the name of the client is spelled wrong. What would you do?"

Pat: That sounds like a big problem. But I would want to know more information. Was this done through a vendor or in-house? How important is the presentation? I guess I am different because I do ask questions!"

Interviewer's thoughts: I like her questions. She's not making assumptions. She could work out.

7. "So what makes you think you are qualified for this position? You don't seem to be?"

This question is designed to provoke a response. The response the interviewer is looking for is not the answer but how you react to confrontation and conflict. You need to pick two or three main ideas about the job, and about yourself, and connect them. It's a good idea to target the skills that are directly related to the position and then provide a brief story to show your success in the past. Don't get combative with the employer, but prove your worth.

Interviewer: "I get that you have some background but I really want someone who has a lot of experience working in a fast-paced environment. Are you up to it?"

Pat: "Yes. Sometimes people don't get me. It's something I've found. I guess I work really hard and don't brag about it. That's a problem I guess."

Interviewer's thoughts: I don't know. Pat's a bit prickly. I don't know.

Interviewer: "I get that you have some background but I really want someone who has a lot of experience working in a fast-paced environment. Are you up to it?"

Pat: "Yes. Yes, I am. In my last job I worked for five managers. They all had projects with tough deadlines. I often had to work late nights and weekends. I guess I'm different I don't get upset by things. I grew up in a big family!"

Interviewer's thoughts: Pat's got what I need. Yep.

8. "Where do you see yourself in five or 10 years' time?"

On a beach in Mexico...no, just kidding. Make your goals realistic. Too much ambition does not look good in an interview. Promotions usually come in one to three years so work with that. Don't talk about your outsider dreams that don't relate to work and then give the interviewer the impression you are not committed or going to stay.

Interviewer: "So where do you see yourself in five years?"

Pat: "That's a good question. I love my work but I also like my hobbies. I am a poet and so I never know when I am going to sell a poem or get a book. It's exciting to think about. And I would love to teach kids to write poetry."

Interviewer's thoughts: A poet? She is not going to fit in.

And let's see another way of answering this question.

Interviewer: "So where do you see yourself in five years?"
Pat: "That's a good question. I love my work so I hope that I would still be working here but always learning new things and challenging myself."
Interviewer's thoughts: I think she could fit in.

9. "Why should we hire you for this position?"

You need to summarize your skills in a way that is directly relevant to what you have learned about the position in the interview. Be thoughtful, be organized, and be genuine. Make sure you stress how you are different in a way that is a positive not a negative.

Pat: "I have ten years experience working with executives providing support including sales presentations. I have traveled extensively so I understand foreign cultures will be helpful in your business. I also understand design and business. That's a rare combination and it will make a big difference in the work I do."

10. "Is there anything you would like to know about the company?"

This is often the last question asked. It's a good idea to have a few questions prepared regarding the position and the potential for growth. Leave questions about vacation time and pay raise at home. You want to get offered the job before you get into specifics. You should do your research on vacation time, pay, and other benefits with HR, the recruiter and with other people in the industry.

Pat: "I'd be interested in hearing where you think the company is going in the next five years. I'm really interested in the foreign business you are working on."
Interviewer: "I expect to expand more into Latin America."

When Does the Interview Start?

Don't think that the interview only starts once you meet the recruiter or the employer in that nice conference room at their site. The interview begins as soon as you apply for the job.

Once you apply, the recruiter or employer will be looking at applications and will see who they want to move forward with. The first step is often a phone screening interview. So beware. If the phone rings and it shows some number you've never seen, don't immediately assume that it's another telemarketer or someone asking for a contribution to freedom for whales or foreign missionaries. It could be your friendly recruiter checking you out.

So don't do as I have done:

"Hi, can I speak to David Couper?"

"I'm not interested, and please put me on your do-not-call list." Slam down phone.

Be Prepared—Always

Whoops! Have a list of who you have applied to, a copy of the resume you sent them (if you're smart you use different versions depending on the position requirements), and any research you've done, by the phone so you can be ready! Once you get over the initial surprise then it's just plain sailing through the normal interview questions. The screening interview is usually trying to find out if you are good match and if there is anything that is going to be a barrier—salary, travel, relocation, and so on.

An alternative approach is, if you are not calm and prepared (it might have been three months since you applied), say "I am just walking out the door for an appointment, can we schedule a time to talk tomorrow, or this week?" Of course you run the risk with this approach that the employer goes to the next candidate and doesn't call back.

Let's say the screening interview goes well and you are asked in to meet with the big cheeses.

Watch Your Ps and Qs

Remember it's showtime as soon as you leave your home, and even more so when you are at the employer's location. Don't spit in the parking lot. Don't swear at the receptionist. Don't swipe at a fly with the company's annual report. I have known potential employees not to get a job because they took their frustrations out on the guy or gal at reception and that person shared it with his or her long-time friend, the CEO.

All these lapses are unintentional, but sometimes employers are deliberate about catching you with your guard down. The walk from the lobby to the interview room, the ride on the elevator, or the tour of the factory floor are all great places to get you off guard. This is where the employer asks you questions about how your outsider style will work out in this insider culture. "Be a big change for you working in a messed-up mega company like ours after working on your own." Or he slips in the follow up question about the gap in your career history, which you so skillfully deflected earlier: "So the time when you were studying for your project management certificate? That was really after you got laid off and it took you a while to get your next gig, right?" Or even the illegal question they have been dying to ask, "How many kids do you have? Four? Wow, that must make overnight trips real tough—who babysits?"

Follow Up

Once you get back home, having avoided road rage or subway spats, you can relax. Well, you can relax once you have sent a follow-up or thank-you note. This confirms how perfectly matched you are for the job, answers any issues or problems that came up and thanks the interviewer for his or her time. It can be an e-mail or a snail mail approach.

E-mail is fast and arrives while you are still fresh on the interviewer's mind. The snail mail, especially if it's a handwritten card, gives the interviewer an insight into who you are and what makes you a successful outsider. You may be surprised to hear that for many HR professionals not sending a thank-you note or follow-up card is a big no-no and can result in you being thrown out of the running in favor of someone with better understanding of protocol.

Even after you land the job, and you have finished your 90-day probationary period, you are still being "interviewed" by the people with whom you work. Remember that, and you will do well!

Presentations

Sometimes, as part of the interview process or to win a consulting gig, you will need to make a presentation. According to one survey, people fear making a presentation more than dying. That's a bit extreme! Think of making a presentation as having a conversation with more than one person. Most of the same things that apply to having a conversation (making it interesting and motivating) apply to a presentation, but more so. Here's what I mean.

Presentation skills

As an outsider you may want to take an innovative approach to getting a job by doing a presentation. If you are a freelancer or starting a business, you will need to make a presentation. A presentation is simply how you sell a concept which can be you, your project, or your business product or service. In a job interview you might make a presentation to explain what you would do if you got the job. This can impress a potential employer if your presentation is good, and it shows you understand the target company. It is doubly impressive if making presentations will be a part of your job. Here are some things to think about:

Know yourself, what you can offer an organization, how you add value—your unique selling proposition. If you are a consultant or running a business, know the service or product that you sell and show that you bring qualities and talents that make you a cut above the mainstream, while supporting the mainstream needs of the client or customer.

One of my most successful presentations was to a healthcare company. My audience had years of experience in the industry. At the time I had never worked in healthcare. The value I could bring this company was not my healthcare knowledge but my deep experience in training and development in *other* industries. I could offer the company a new perspective on training and development based on other businesses. This was unique as it was the first time my audience had heard someone outside of their industry. The presentation went well because I was not tied into their old stories about the ways things had to be.

Know your audience. Half of winning is advance research and preparation. Know whether your crowd is into details or broad concepts, facts or fables, slide or story. Seek what they really need, what it will take to put you over the top while your competition is clumped together in one mass of sameness with the same perspective and same common or well-worn solutions. And of course know why they will react to your possibly eccentric take on their needs.

Rehearse. It always helps to rehearse your presentation. If you don't have a willing friend or colleague, tape it and replay it to yourself the next day. It certainly is important to have a sense of timing to ensure you cover all your wonderful information and leave time for Q&A. But also remember the next point.

Read your audience. Many presenters have their presentation down pat. It's polished and perfect and boring! If there is no real connection, the audience dozes off. If you don't see when the audience has questions, is confused, or loves what you're saying you're missing the chance for real discussion during which you bond with your audience. Don't overlook this in favor of sticking to your rehearsed speech.

Know the room. Know where your audience will sit and where you will stand. Check out the audience's view to see if there are any "limited view" seats. Know where any key stakeholders will be so that you can talk to them at key moments in the presentation. Get all equipment set up and have a back-up plan if the projector goes down (printed copies) or your laptop can't read your corrupted disk (a duplicate disk).

Now let's look at writing a winning proposal and the three Proposal Pointers: Connecting, Providing Solutions, and Showcasing Your Uniqueness.

1. Connecting

The most important thing about writing a proposal is connecting with the client or customer. That means you need to understand the business, provide a solution that will meet its needs, and show yourself as unique and different from the common competition.

To understand the business you need to research. Find out as much as possible from as many different sources as possible. As an outsider, you have the ability to see things differently from the client and differently from your competition, and that has added value.

For example, I was once asked to give a proposal to a company on how to train its employees on policies and procedures. In the proposal, I showed that I understood the problem—policies and procedures are vital to do the work correctly and consistently, but they were not viewed as interesting or important. I showed my expertise when I described how the company could use video, online training, and a workbook to deliver the solution. But I also showed my outsider skills. I like to make people laugh, and in training humor can go a long way. But many trainers are scared of being funny. They don't want to take the risk of offending someone. I took the risk and came up with a skit that showed what would happen if we didn't have policies and procedures in an everyday situation such as checking in at the airport. I created a scene whereby the person at the check-in asks for identification, but in one case it's a passport, in another a birth certificate, and in another a library card. It worked because people could connect to the situation—they had all been there—and laugh at the satire of it, because they could connect to how that could happen. I got the work as a result of my proposal.

2. Providing solutions

You can't provide solutions unless you understand what the problems are. Doing your research is vital to uncover the issues not only with the industry from a global perspective, but also at that particular company.

It's about asking questions. One of my favorites is, "Why now?" Why is the company asking you to work with them at this particular point in time? That is a key question, and if you don't know the answer, you can find your proposal to be at a devastating disadvantage. But the solution needs to showcase why you are different. This is what will win you the job.

I once created a proposal for a change management program for a utilities company. The issue was that there had been a reorganization and as a result people did not trust each other and work together. The solution was to introduce and discuss a change management model, which helped people to express their feelings and work through them. But I added a twist by having a group of actors play out common scenarios the employees were experiencing. Because I had written plays and was experienced in the theater I could write and direct the scenes. This was a very different solution than the average consultant would have offered. It got the deal done.

3. Showcasing your uniqueness

Why should the client work with you as opposed to any other Tom, Dick, or Harriet? Because you're unique. Because you are the only one who offers greater value, can get the best results, head and shoulders above the rest. Because you have an outsider view of the inside problem.

For example, I put in a proposal for doing work as a coach with a U.S. company. They had some issues with personnel in their Tokyo office. They needed someone to coach the managers on how to be more effective but they also wanted someone who could understand the Japanese culture. I was that person. My outsider experience paid off and helped to get the work.

GOING IT ALONE: SELF-EMPLOYMENT

For many outsiders, the best possible career change involves self-employment. In this chapter we're going to look at how to extend the lessons of being a successful outsider to becoming an entrepreneur.

We've been assuming so far that you want a new job, but actually there is another option. You can choose to go freelance or start your own business. For many outsiders, being able to work independently and be in charge is hugely appealing. After all, who could possibly be a better boss to work for than yourself? For some, this is true; for others, not so much. And for many, it is something we just learn to grow into.

Being Your Own Boss

One of my clients in the entertainment business took the big step and went out on her own. In her words, this is how it happened.

> *Friends had often said to me that after 20 years in the business, I had the relationships and the skills to go out on my own. I enjoyed working with clients in the international markets, and it was a new interesting area for me.*

Over dinner one night, a former favorite UK client told me he was starting his own company, and he hoped, as this developed, we could work together again. My assistant quit and said he was going to teach film at a prep school in South America. I was envious of both of them and their new endeavors.

With guidance from an excellent coach, I stumbled into signing a few clients on retainer, and I set up my own consulting business in international sales and packaging. I feel valued and respected by my clients. There is no one checking to see if I am clocking in every day. I work longer hours and face administrative challenges of being an entrepreneur. I am engaged in an adventure with a future and feel better about myself and my expanding skills and knowledge.

—Pat, Former Sales Executive, Consultant, Entertainment Industry, Los Angeles, California

Your Own Business—What Does It Take?

If you run your own business, you can decide your own schedule, your own dress code, and you are totally free to be yourself, theoretically. Even if you are working alone you will still need to work with clients, and that probably means following some of their practices. So if you decide your schedule will be to work from 4 p.m. until 2 a.m., you may find some of your local customers don't like that arrangement. But this may work perfectly for international buyers. Bingo! You have transformed an outsider problem into an outsider advantage. Likewise, you may love to wear your PJs at home for work. Great. If you never meet your clients it's a perfect option. If you do, then think again. Unless you are Hugh Heffner, founder of the Playboy Empire, who commonly wears pajamas and a robe for business, it's not going to fly. But you definitely want to be yourself. That's your unique selling proposition.

How do you do business on your own? Defining your options

Before we jump into this let's look at some definitions. What does it mean to have your own business? Or to be self-employed? Are they the same or different?

Business types

Legally, the main types of business are: Self Employed as a Sole proprietor or an Independent Contractor; Partnership; Corporation.

Keep in mind that as a consultant, for example, you could set your consultancy up in any of these structures depending on your tax, client, liability, and numerous other considerations.

One warning. I am not a lawyer! Laws vary from town to town, state to state, country to country *and* they change. What I write is from a U.S. perspective, but you must check with a lawyer or other legal profession-al before starting your own business in whatever form that takes. That means confirming your own personal situation with professionals, and its best to do that at the start, not six months later after having chosen a structure without adequate deliberation.

Self-employed

You are self-employed if you have a business you run to make a profit. The business does not have to be full-time. Being self-employed can mean that you sell products or services. It also includes being free-lance or an independent contractor.

If you have a business selling socks at the swap meet you will be self employed. That is, any money you make—the profit—after you pay for the materials, rent of a space at the meet, gas to get you there, and so on, will be yours. You employ yourself and pay yourself. And you can be self-employed even if you only do this on Sundays and you work at Acme Co. from Monday to Friday.

Partnership

Depending on how you do business, it gets a little bit more compli-cated. If you are a sole proprietor, that means you do business as yourself, by yourself, and for yourself. Legally you and the business are the same. A partnership is similar except you and your partners are the business.

A note on being in partnership: If you choose other outsiders they may drive you nuts because when they do something wrong you know exactly why they did that. You can see yourself in them. If you choose insiders they may drive you nuts because when they do something wrong you have no clue why they did that. You can't see yourself in them, and that is very disturbing. Whoever you choose, be sure you understand where they are coming from and how they complement you.

Corporation or limited liability partnership

Now when you set up a corporation or a limited liability partnership (LLP) you and the business are not the same. The huge difference is that in a sole proprietorship or a partnership the debts of the business are also your debts.

What does that mean? It means that if you have a coffee shop as a sole proprietorship and one of your customers sues you for something you did wrong—like a bug in their blueberry muffin you made and sold them—they could sue you for all the business *and* your personal assets. So they could get the tables and chairs in the coffee shop and the tables and chairs in your apartment—and your car, home, and savings and retirement accounts. Depending on your business and personal net worth, think carefully about this track.

If you operate as the Coffee Shop, Inc. then your liability (how much you could be asked to pay in the bug case) would be limited to all the company's assets (the items your coffee shop owned). Normally, your personal items would be safe, excluded, unless you had done something illegal and then the courts might decide you deserve to lose your couch and big-screen TV.

Be sure you have the best tax situation and legal structure for your business. Talk to professionals such as lawyers or accountants who are experienced in small-business matters. The folks at SCORE.org, a wonderful group of volunteers who help would-be business owners get going, can be a great resource, and check with your state for local programs and assistance. Be sure you get this stuff right from the start and avoid potential problems down the road!

Sell your uniqueness and let your advisors or clients work out the details

The best structure for your business, and the best terms for a particular contract, depend on a number of factors, which will vary. When in doubt, talk to your attorney, accountant, or small business consulting expert *before* negotiating details of a contract, and just consider that (deductible) expense a cost of doing business.

Limiting beliefs about self-employment

Many people—outsiders especially who already doubt their abilities—buy in to common misconceptions about running a business or being freelance, especially compared with having a job, which is something most people know a lot more about. Those beliefs tend to be limiting, and although it is understandable to have concerns, or fears, about running your own company or going freelance, it's important that whatever decision you may make about going into business for yourself be based on accurate information. And remember, most successful entrepreneurs had those very same doubts, and, to be sure, many experienced setbacks and failures on their road to success.

> *Entrepreneurs in particular seem prone to feeling on top of the world one minute, only to feel crushed by it the next.*
> *To this breed, I assure you all: in our species, it's normal.*
> *It's an integral part of building anything remarkable, whether a business, a relationship, or a life.*
> —Tim Ferris, *Four Hour Work Week*
> *www.fourhourworkweek.com/blog/2009/01/12/nick-vijicic-get-back-up/*

When counseling clients on career issues and goals, going into business for one's self is a topic that most should seriously evaluate at some time in their life, even if it is only to determine that it is not in their best interest. Armed with that conclusion, they can go back to focusing on their employment—and enjoying it more—instead of day-dreaming about the greener grass on the other side of the fence. On self-employment, the most common misperceptions that arise, and the corresponding reality, are summarized in the following three Business Belief Busters.

Three Business Belief Busters

1. Most businesses fail or make no money.
2. You're more secure in a job than working for yourself.
3. I'm not disciplined enough to be out on my own.

1. Most businesses fail or make no money.

Well. Some businesses fail and some businesses do not make money. Depending on the type of business and location, those statistics can vary enormously. The success of the business depends primarily on you. If you are experienced, knowledgeable, and do your homework about your new business and how to run it, your probabilities of success are much higher. It's up to you how much effort you put into the business. Having said that, there is always risk unknown factors that can make or break you.

From French Fancies to French Fries

My parents, having given up careers in the corporate world, led an outsider life, running businesses. They bought a run-down restaurant and decided to open it as a teashop selling little cakes and cookies. The restaurant was in the old part of town surrounded by antique shops. My mother loved to bake and they had already owned a hotel so they were used to catering. They expected that the shoppers at the antique stores would come in for a little lunch or afternoon tea after an exhausting couple of hours messing around with 18th-century teapots or Betty Boop memorabilia or pre-war Japanese buttons. Initially, the restaurant was a mess, including a trail of grease from the kitchen in back to the counter up front. It looked like someone had carried a dripping basket of French fries from back to front. But my parents fixed it all up, including the grease trap, and opened for business.

Unfortunately the plan did not work out. The rich antique collectors got in their cars and drove home or to some other place. Instead my parents found that their customers were students from the local college. They soon had to change plans and became a diner serving burgers and fries, making a healthy profit.

Their first attempt failed but their second one—with new, more current operating data available and properly analyzed—succeeded.

And what do the statistics say?

"Seven out of 10 new employer firms survive at least two years, and about half survive five years."

This is from the Small Business Administration, and the odds are fair: a 50/50 chance of success after five years. The numbers can be read as positive or negative depending on your attitude—glass half full or half empty. At least half of businesses make it. Your level of risk tolerance, and your success, is up to you.

2. You're more secure in a job than working for yourself.

I may be the wrong person to ask about this! I've been laid off three times. The first time I thought I was going to be given a bonus by my boss but actually he was holding on to a piece of paper, while ashen-faced he read some legalese about how I was getting dumped because there wasn't enough work in the company. Western corporate culture has never felt less loyalty to its employees than when quarterly results and shareholders are on the line. But *your* position, for whatever reason, may actually be highly secure. In some ways, you may have more security working for yourself and be more in control. You can make the calls, do the meet-and-greets to find new clients, rather than relying on other people, who, you probably don't know. Of course you don't know about the direction of the economy, but having a job doesn't insulate you or your company from economic risk either.

There are career assessments such as Campbell Interest and Skill Survey (CISS) or personality assessments such as Gallup's Strengths-Finder 2.0 and even Watson-Glaser II Critical Thinking Appraisal, which assesses your thinking ability.

Another way of going is to try it out. Have a garage sale and see how well you do. Sell some collectibles online. Make cookies and sell them at your office. Or you can listen to your heart, not your head and the fear floating around it.

If you realize that selling is not for you then you can choose to be happily employed doing what you do well, team up with a business partner who excels in new business development, or hire someone else who is. No entrepreneur wears all the hats well, and the most successful recognize and leverage their talents, while being good at identifying and hiring others with complementary talents.

> *I definitely feel more secure as a solo entrepreneur, than being subject to the whims of some other entity. If I build my network and take care of my clients, it's the best job security there is.*
> —Steve Woodruff, entrepreneur

Comment on article about running a small business on Business-week.com   *www.businessweek.com/smallbiz/running_small_business/archives/2009/08/entrepreneurs_a.html*

Outsiders can be very good entrepreneurs. If you struggle with the uncertainty then get a business coach, mentor, or experienced partner to guide you through the traps.

I'm not disciplined enough to be out on my own.

This could be! Many people find that without the structure of a boss and deadlines they may be challenged in this regard. I have worked with clients who decided to go out on their own, but gave up on that career choice because they found out that they needed the routine of a job to be productive. It depends on who you are and it depends on the type of business. Outsiders sometimes find structure difficult so this belief could be true of you. But outsiders do well with project work.

If you are the kind of person who finds it hard to get things done on the weekends, or if your garage project has been on hold for the last 10 years, or you just hating making plans during your free time, you may find it hard to run your own business. Or not. You may find that actually when you are working for yourself and are driven for success that the planning, organization, and dependability you were lacking in your personal projects will magically appear in your own business.

Again, if you don't know, try it out. Start something small on the side, perhaps on the Internet, and see how it goes operating on evenings and weekends. Help out a friend who has a business for a couple of weeks and see how you get on. Take a six-month sabbatical and live on your savings to see if your dream is delightful or dire.

It's all about passion and drive!

> *The main quality that you have to have to start your own business is a burning desire to do it…You have to really, really want to be your own boss, transform your dream into reality, or market your product or service.*
> —Susan Ward, *Thinking of Starting a Small Business? About.com*
> *http://sbinfocanada.about.com/cs/startup/a/startownbiz.htm*

Busted the Business Belief Busters? Now What?

If you have worked though the Business Belief Busters, and you are set on running your own business, then there are probably many competing thoughts of risks, obstacles, rewards, and more going through your mind. All those issues will not be resolved today—you need to give yourself time to plan and then take baby steps to achieve your dream. But today is a good time to consider some principles to follow. These principles will help you honor who you are as an outsider as well as become a successful, self-employed businessperson!

These seven principles or standards have worked well for me as a businessperson, and, especially, as a successful outsider.

Seven standards for success

1. Focus and Intention: If you go on a two-week trip and you are not focused on your destination, you may have fun exploring different places and experiencing different cultures, but you may also spend all your time lost in inner-city decay and dull landscapes, or going past the same McDonalds time after time. If you have no plan, and no goal, it's difficult to know if you have achieved anything.

> *One of the biggest causes of failure is diffusion of focus, Grousbeck says. The first year you should have two over-arching goals: meeting or exceeding your projections and treating your customers right.*
> —Elizabeth Kountze, *Six Steps to Starting Your Own Business*, quoting H. Irving Grousbeck, co-director of the Center for Entrepreneurial Studies at Stanford Business School. This article was originally written in 2006 by Elizabeth Kountze. It was updated in May 2008.

In business, I have found that if you have no focus, you can often dilute your energy working on many different ideas and opportunities. I know a great woman who is a trainer, a speaker, a consultant, a social worker, a therapist, a major volunteer, and a very tired lady! She makes some progress in one area and then something else shows up that demands her attention. She is always busy, so she is always missing appointments and meetings.

Why does she have this divergent focus? I don't know but I can guess that part of it is that she loves all of it and finds it hard to choose. I also believe that she is worried that she may pick the wrong thing to focus on, so she needs to protect herself by doing a bunch of things. It could be that she is fearful. She is fearful of not making enough money, not being noticed, or not doing enough. So that makes her want to cram as many things in her day as possible.

Sometimes we get seduced by the idea that multitasking is ideal, that we can do many different things at the same time and to the same standard of excellence. The media also makes us buy in to this myth. Many celebrities seem to do many things. They act, they direct, they produce, and then they write a book on how to decorate your house in Shabby Chic. But here is a reality check. They didn't start out doing all of these things at the same time. They usually were successful in one area first and then moved into other work. Obviously, if you are doing well in one area you are likely to be taken more seriously in a related area. So the actor becomes a director—but not usually at the same time, and not without help. If you are highly successful in a number of areas you are probably not doing your own cleaning, cooking, shopping, or even your own comedy—you have a joke writer. Get successful in one area and then take on another. If you can't decide, then just pick one. If it doesn't work out go on to the next. The indecision or the attempt to do many things at the same time will only backfire.

2. Your Intention Is Important. If you go into a venture with unclear intentions you will get unclear results. Setting intentions means stating what you are looking for in your business. But don't confuse this with, or get caught up in, goals. Intentions are different. *I intend to spend time with my family* is an intention. A goal is, *I will go to Disneyland with my family.* You can achieve your goal or not. Nothing wrong with that; we need goals, but they are also limited. An intention is different; it is not limited. *I intend to spend time with my family* is an ongoing desire. It is something that lasts longer than a trip to a theme park. The intention is a way of being.

When life appears to be working against you, when your luck is down, when the supposedly wrong people show up, or when you slip up and return to old, self-defeating habits, recognize the signs that you're out of harmony with intention.
—Aldous Huxley (1894–1963)

It is important to set intentions that are aligned with your heart. Your intentions should not be about what your head is saying. For example, *I intend to be rich and famous* sounds like your head talking. It's what your parents might have said to you! *I intend to write a book in which I share my experience of being a single mother so that I can help others* is an intention from your heart. An intention can motivate and inspire you.

3. You're the Boss—Manage Your Time: In a job, your time is managed, but when self-employed you must manage your own schedule without failing at the tasks or burning out. Structure and your schedule can depend on what kind of business you do. My parents had a bed and breakfast. That is an ultimate 24/7 job. When the guests are not eating, they are messing up the place (I mean enjoying their stay) so that you need to clean. While they sleep, you are getting ready to do it all again the next day and finding your new guests. It's not a fun and leisurely activity, except in the books about the adventurers who buy a wreck in the Berkshires, Bahamas, or Bahai and have an instant success.

If you open a retail store, you will have hours you need to be open. Not much problem being organized there. Unless you hate working through lunch and being busy every evening catching up with the day's books, inventory, ordering, and marketing. But if you open a business on the Internet where there are no opening and closing hours, you may either end up working non-stop selling or, worse, working 24/7 on marketing, researching, networking, and keeping up on current trends. Another possibility is that you are distracted and don't work on your business. You work every waking hour on watching TV, texting, and talking with buddies. I know one outsider, a successful freelancer writer, who confessed that she hadn't read a book in a year. Reading was supposed to be one of her hobbies but there always seemed to be something to do in her career that prevented her from keeping her personal life in balance. Remember, you're the boss, and if keeping your life in balance is an intention, and it isn't happening, you need to re-evaluate your priorities and operating style.

Changing a career track from an employee to self-employed entails drastic life changes. Everything shifts 180 degrees, including the way you manage time.
—Isabel Isidro, Managing Editor, PowerHomeBiz.com
www.powerhomebiz.com/vol143/time.htm

So how can you be sure that you can deal with issues with working on your own and managing your time effectively?

If you are not sure if self-employment and its time-management challenges suits you, research and sample different types of businesses. Work part time in a store during the holiday season. Help out a friendly entrepreneur for a couple of weekends. Read about small business successes, or autobiographies of successful entrepreneurs—this topic has a whole section at the bookstore. Network to or approach local business owners in which you have interest and ask them to mentor you, in exchange for some of your time helping out, so you can get a first-hand look.

4. Marketing Is Not Optional. Often businesspeople don't plan their marketing, it just happens. That can work, but it can also fail. It makes sense to plan marketing. But how?

A useful method is to weigh the impact alongside the cost, and factor in your outsider uniqueness in determining the potential benefit. For example, say you open a restaurant, the first vegetarian fast-food joint—soy burgers and soy tenders. (Hey, it could work...)

Marketing Method	Cost	Impact	Outsider Factor
Print media	$$$	Wide, but may not have high results.	Something different could catch on big!
Fliers	$	Limited, but could have good results if targeted.	Each flier tells your story of how you lost 40 pounds by only eating veggies.

TV Advert	$$$$$	Really wide, but not cost effective unless you obtain cheaper local cable rates.	You use your "big" personality and dress up like a beanburger.
Free tastings	$$	Limited, but effective for local customers.	Healthy can taste great! Once in, great food and your winning personality ensures customers return.

Marketing can take many forms these days, including social media such as Twitter, Facebook, or YouTube.

When J.R. Cohen, Operations Manager for CoffeeGroundz (http://twitter.com/coffeegroundz) Cafe in Houston, Texas first heard about Twitter from one of his customers, he was puzzled but intrigued. Today, he credits Twitter with almost doubling his clientele and with opening his eyes to a whole new way to build community.
—Erica O'Grady, Chief Experience Officer
http://peanutbuttermedia.com/
Writing on Mr. Tweet's Blog
http://blog.mrtweet.net/twitter-to-go-how-one-local-coffee-shop-used-twitter-to-double-his-clientele

What does doing something remarkable mean? It means getting noticed. It means doing something that is a risk. It means acting from your heart.

5. Be Businesslike: This sounds silly. But many businesspeople, especially outsiders, don't run their business like a business. Having a business means you make money. If you don't, then that's a nonprofit organization or a charity. So when you give your goods or services away without getting paid for them, you are breaking the first rule of being a business.

Sometimes outsiders get confused about this. They were working in business when they realize, that their calling is healing, but then think that they shouldn't charge for this work or they shouldn't charge too much. That's not a good conversation to be having with yourself. If you have a business you need to make money, period—end of story. If not, it's a hobby.

> *Gregg Steiner, for example, was always helping techno pho-*
> *bic friends and family members set up their computers and Ti-*
> *Vos and cell phones and plasma TVs for the fun of it. Then, last*
> *summer, a friend of a friend offered to pay him to wire his huge*
> *house in Los Angeles. And Steiner soon left his family's baby-*
> *ointment manufacturing company in Cleveland to turn his geek-*
> *dom into a lucrative consultancy. "Now I'm getting paid $95 an*
> *hour and I get all these perks, and I'm busy all the time and just*
> *having fun," says the 35-year-old Steiner.*
> *—www.startupnation.com/articles/1180/1/AT_Turning-*
> *Hobby-Into-Business.asp.* (Reproduced with Permission.)

Along with this cardinal profit rule are a number of others that support you in making money. You need to keep your promises. You need to meet your customers' expectations. You need to give good value. And so on. And what does this translate to? You can't just rely on being different and unique, you also need to deliver—to get the orders out on time, sell what you say you will sell, and be fair to your staff, your customers and yourself.

6. The Customer Is Not Always Right, but He or She Is Always the Customer: A customer can be completely wrong, but they will still be the customer who has the power to make or break a deal. So I have learned that the customer is always the customer, even when he or she is wrong! With such customers, the trick is to say no while actually saying yes, and making them, and you, happy. Easy, right? So, I'm working with a coaching client and he says, "I need a new resume today—it's got to be completely written." So I have a number of choices. I can say:

1. "No, I can get it done in 48 hours. That's the normal time frame."
2. "Of course."
3. "Of course. I can expedite it, and there will be an additional $100 charge."
4. "Tell me more about what you need."

Option A gets the client pissed off. Option B gets me irritated. Option C could get both of us pissed off— the work still has to be produced, in a rush, and the client has to pay more and he doesn't understand that's how it works. Option D is the best option, as we will now see:

Resume Client: "Well, I have a good friend who told me to send him my resume so he can talk to his boss about me."

Me: "Okay, I get it. That sounds like a great opportunity. What concerns me is that we rush the resume and it's not up to standard. It isn't fair to you or to your friend. If he thinks it has problems, he won't pass it on to his boss."

Resume Client: "Yes. You make a couple of good points. But I need to do something."

Me: "Exactly! So why not talk to him and find out more about what his company is looking for? Spend some time talking to him and answering his questions. That way, he will be much better prepared to talk to his boss than if you give him a resume. "

Resume Client: "But he doesn't have a lot of time."

Me: "So you don't want to waste it. You can tell your friend that if he just sends a resume, you're worried that his boss is going to have a number of questions he won't be able to answer. So it's better to give him the information up front."

Resume Client: "I guess that makes sense. But what about the resume?"

Me: "You tell your friend that we can get his boss the resume after he's talked to him."

Resume Client: "Okay, that makes sense. Thanks, you always are so responsive. I appreciate it."

A no became a yes. Everyone was happy. It was the best solution.

7. Not Every Customer Is the Right Customer: This may seem strange, but not every customer is for you. You want the customers who love you, pay on time and in full, and don't complain. If your customers don't do that, then you either aren't doing a good job of running your business, or you have the wrong customers.

Early on in my career, I was doing some coaching for a company that found the clients who then outsourced the work to me. It was a good plan and initially it worked out fine. The clients were great. I was enjoying myself and it was going well. Then things started to go badly. I submitted my invoices, and they didn't get paid on time. I called...and nothing. I called again, and still nothing. I finally got paid. I was asked to work on a project, turned down other work, and then found it was cancelled before it started. Again my invoices didn't get paid on time. So in the end, even though I needed the business, I finally said no. I liked the company, I liked the clients, and I understood they had money problems, but in the end I had to stop ignoring what my intuition was telling me. As soon as I started to listen to what my heart was saying things in my business turned around for the better. I was retained by new clients on better terms. I realized I had to value myself and in the end just say no.

Have Fun. Although this sounds easy, some people find their lives become their business, or worse, their business becomes their lives. Instead of enjoying their work, and their free time, they find that there is nothing but the business. It becomes an addiction constantly needing to be fed.

Of course you can have fun at work, all the more so if you have your own business. But some outsiders seem to forget that. This may be because they found their dream work and they don't want to miss anything, or they forget how to relax and kick back a little, afraid the customers may not be there next week or next month. They become consumed, all about business, 24/7. Worse, they may think their customers and clients are like that too.

Clients don't necessary like to work every weekend or talk about business at every meeting. They might rather play a round of golf, or discuss their kids or favorite sports team, instead of talking about productivity or process. It's important to bond with clients at multiple levels, not just business. And, ultimately, it's all about finding balance. If finding balance seems like a daily struggle, don't worry, that's common, and a good sign that you are aware of and seeking balance.

Working on your own is not for everyone. I have had clients who have great success freelancing, and others who choose to stay "corporate" and have been equally happy and effective in that world. But for those who love being an entrepreneur, they could never imagine doing anything else! For many outsiders, going freelance or into business for yourself is a great choice.

10

OVERCOMING BARRIERS TO SUCCESS

We've looked at tools and strategies that make an outsider successful in the workplace, but you may still be facing challenges or barriers.

At times, you may doubt who you are, feel afraid, or be unwilling to risk being rejected for your uniqueness. At that point, you have to look to the passion that drives you, the spirit that keeps you alive, and the joy available to you simply for living your truth. Be yourself even if—especially if—that makes you different, and keep working toward greater success however you define it. The alternative is to live as if you were already dead—taking your passion from other people's dreams.

> *Most people are other people. Their thoughts are someone else's opinions, their lives a mimicry, their passions a quotation.*
> —Oscar Wilde, De Profundis, 1905; Irish dramatist, novelist, and poet (1854–1900)

Make Fear Your Friend!

Fear is probably the biggest issue. We are afraid of what we don't know. We are afraid that we might make a mistake and someone will punish us or we will look stupid. We are even afraid that we might be successful. That may be because we fear stepping out of the shadows and into the limelight. Or we may feel guilty that we are successful and other people are not. Or even that if we are a success we won't be able to stand the pressure of being on top. Fear is a killer. We doubt ourselves. We doubt other people. We doubt the world. Fear is not something to be overcome. It is something that we should notice, use when appropriate, and ignore when it does not serve us. You are right to be scared to jump out of a plane without a parachute. You have a right to be scared by your boss, by interviews, and by cold-calling.

Sometimes we have to go back to basics and do some more work on fundamentals.

Five Outsider Traits Revisited

Do you remember the Five Outsider Traits that were introduced in Chapter 1? We can use these as a way to look at what is holding us back or tripping us up.

1. Outsiders look different.
2. Outsiders sound different.
3. Outsiders act different.
4. Outsiders feel different.
5. Outsiders are made to feel different.

Sometimes these signifiers can become barriers and end up as long-term challenges.

Let's look at each factor separately, and discuss what we can do to overcome and turn them to our advantage.

Factor 1: Outsiders look different.

We know that outsiders can look different because of ethnicity, disability, or other physical features.

The one young, single, female supervisor in a manufacturing company whom I coached had very little in common with her male colleagues who were older and married with kids. She was literally half their size, and, unlike her white, Hispanic, and African American colleagues, she was Asian. She was an outsider and found it tough to succeed.

Working in a Japanese company as a teacher of English, I didn't look like my colleagues. Aside from the obvious (they were Asian and Japanese and I was white and British), I was also much taller at 6 feet 2 inches. As I walked the halls of the company, I was greeted constantly with "Takai desus ne!" At first I thought it was a normal greeting, roughly translating to *How's it going?* After six months, I realized the phrase translated as "Isn't he tall!" I was identified as different.

What can we do to cope with looking different?

- Blend in.
- Embrace the different look.

Coping strategies

Wearing the uniform can be a good thing: Blend in. What I mean is that when you wear the same clothes as your colleagues, you also make yourself look similar to your colleagues. But just because you are wearing the uniform doesn't mean that you are the same as everyone else, or that you have sold out. Internally, you will still be different, and that's fine. Going with the accepted dress code in an organization means that your employer can focus on what makes you unique and valuable, not what makes you unique and not fit in. Why argue about your fashion sense, when you can be embracing your differences that will be marketable and sought after? Fighting about wearing sweats as business casual, your wacky tie, or your revealing neckline seems like energy wasted. Dress to blend in; work to stand out.

For example, the female Asian supervisor at the manufacturing company made the choice to look like one of the guys. She wore overalls, safety boots, and a baseball cap. She didn't wear make-up, her hair was tucked into her hat, and her nails didn't understand the word *manicure*. She could have worn more feminine clothes, and still been successful, but she selected a different route that proved more effective for her. From the back view she could have passed for one of the guys. Instead of making a statement in the way she dressed, she made a statement in how she acted as a supervisor. She chose to focus her energy to fight that battle only, where she could produce the greatest success.

Dress to be noticed: Embrace the different look. Conversely, I took a different but equally effective track when I worked in Japan.

I was tall and I stood out as a foreigner. Instead of trying to fit in, I went out of my way to stand out. Everybody wore suits—dark suits. I also wore suits but had some funky ties from England including one with a picture of the Queen on it. I was a foreigner and I was going to stand out. I was the quintessential British man and I dressed to be recognized as such. By making a statement that I was proud of my Britishness, and comfortable with our differences, I made it easier for my Japanese colleagues to be comfortable with it as well.

Now let's look at the next factor.

Factor 2: Outsiders sound different.

When you have a foreign accent or don't speak the same language, you can find yourself not being part of the group.

One time, in Chicago, I lined up in the company cafeteria for lunch. I asked for a "half sandwich and soup" but the person who was serving couldn't understand what I said with my British accent. I was getting more and more frustrated. Finally, a colleague came to the rescue and told the serving person what I wanted. The serving woman, who was Asian American, sympathized with me saying, "Don't worry, I have trouble with English too." I was an outsider among outsiders! I realized I needed to find a way to cope with this communication breakdowns.

How did I deal with this? With two tactics

- Don't take sounding different too seriously.
- Help them out.

Coping strategies

Laugh and everyone laughs with you: Don't take sounding different too seriously.

Usually, it is best to treat a remark about how different I sound as a joke. Instead of getting upset with the woman in the cafeteria I laughed it off with my colleagues. Sometimes when I get teased about my British accent I either do an American accent back in return, which causes guffaws from my audience, or I over-emphasize my own accent in a

Monty Python style. My theory is that while people are making fun of something as innocent as my accent, they are not worrying about something more serious like why my report is late, or why my fee is twice as much as someone else's!

I am used to people making fun of my British accent. So when my colleagues laughed at me in the cafeteria I was ready to laugh with them to diffuse what was mostly just good-natured kidding. Although, sometimes I feel that if I hear another person say, "Cup of tea" or "Cheerio," with a Dick Van Dyke in *Mary Poppins* accent, I will scream. But they do. And I don't. When they don't get it: help them out.

I deliberately change the way I say some words that can be confusing. I also learn how to switch to a synonym when someone does not understand me. Or I repeat what I have said but with a different accent. It works. Of course some people might argue that I shouldn't need to do that and may be they are right but it seems a small step to make for effective communication and improved relationships.

Sometimes helping them out can include writing something, or using pictures or video to tell the story rather than using your voice if you know you have issues. Or it may be that you get a friend who has a positive and upbeat "newscaster" or standard accent call someone on your behalf or record your phone message.

Factor 3: Outsiders act different

I have sometimes struggled working in a corporate environment, especially those that are male-dominated. I am not that interested in sports, DIY, and cars, which seemed to be the topics that "guys" were interested in. I found myself being (unusually) quiet, withdrawn, and unable to take part in the discussion. I sometimes would find silence when I was with my boss. He was into American Football, action movies, and was a Frat Boy—a guy's guy! His philosophy was that guys should be able to take the tough talk and hard actions. I found that difficult, and I found myself getting quiet, avoiding situations in which I would have to socialize with him, and acting as if I was invisible. I felt that he did not understand me, and I could not act in a real and authentic way.

Coping strategies

Be a good sharer! Just the kids are told to share, we can share too. We can share about ourselves. We can share who we are. That can help us to act differently. We can even share that we feel different. When we share with others, we will find out that they are often feeling the same way or at least they understand our concerns and issues. And even if we find out that people think differently from us, we will both know what each of us is feeling. This sharing will enable us to act differently.

Coping strategies in action

As I said my boss was very different to me. I found that we did not have anything in common which made me act differently. One time I found myself with my boss and began to share with him things about my life in England. He was surprised at some of the things that I told him about the homes there. Then he started talking about homes and one of the programs that he liked on TV, which, strangely enough, was one of my favorites too. I could share my love of architecture and design too. It was a good conversation. I shared that I enjoyed talking about this. And he shared that I often seemed quiet. I shared that I was not that interested in sports. It was all good. The sharing enabled me to act differently.

The lesson here is that we have to share ourselves and find out about others. This information can help you act differently.

Factor 4: Outsiders Feel Different.

When I worked at an accounting firm as a trainer, I felt very different from my boss. Our interests, backgrounds, and even our politics were at opposite ends of the spectrum. He liked programs about gardening and Mrs. Thatcher; I liked foreign films and JFK.

How can we get through this? By finding what we have in common.

Coping strategies

Find common ground and be interested, or even fascinated. We are all the same deep down, and so if you dig a little you will find things that you have in common even with the most unlikely of people.

Conservatives and liberals worry about their kids, listen to Kid Rock, and can even kid each other about their opposite views.

Listening to someone, really listening, can open you up to a very different conversation. If you listen to someone as if he or she is boring, difficult or just plain wrong then that is what you will hear—period. If you are prepared to hear something different you may.

Be open to learn something new. Sometimes you may find that this person you have dismissed actually has great knowledge on a topic of which you have never thought. It may be something that on the surface you don't care much about but, upon a second look, you may discover how much there is to learn. It could be anything from how to train dogs to Civil War history to remodeling kitchens. Be curious!

My accounting firm boss and I were different, but we had some things in common. He had an old house and wonderful gardens. I love architecture, old houses and gardens. If I was to go back to that situation, I would focus on this common ground.

Although we may not seem to have much in common, when we explore, we can always find something in common even if it is small. Or the common ground may not be directly related to the person you are talking to but may include one of his or her family members or friends.

Strangely enough, I had some commonalities with my boss's wife. I like browsing thrift stores for bargains and so did she. It was something small, not directly related to my boss, but it was something, a starting point.

Deep down we have similarities. If we can't see them, then we just need to keep digging until we find them.

Factor 5: Outsiders Are Made to Feel Different.

If you are considered an outsider, people gossip about you. I found that when I worked in Japan, everyone in my department talked about me. They knew I owned a home in England and they thought that was amazing for someone so young. I thought that my home ownership was pretty spectacular too, but that wasn't the point. They knew I had lots of friends and they thought some of them were weird especially the one who had an earring shaped like a pink vampire bat. They knew that I cooked and, yes, they thought that was weird too. The point was that they watched me like I was a reality program where my every movement was scrutinized before reality television had even been created. They made me feel like an outsider.

So how can we cope with being made to feel different?

Coping strategies

Be different and then some. If someone believes you are different, be different and then some—kick it up a few notches. Think of the difference between acting for a film and acting on stage. An actor in a movie makes small gestures, speaks at a normal pitch, and doesn't go over the top in his or her acting style. On stage, an actor must play not only to the front row but also to the balcony. The actor in a play makes big gestures, has to project his or her voice, and may well accentuate the acting style.

If you're being made to feel different, rather than being subtle and discreet, which could suggest you are comfortable with the categorization, you can play to the balcony, make it more noticeable, larger, and bigger. Often people respect you for that because you know who you are and you are not afraid of showing it. So don't hide it, flaunt it!

Coping strategies in action

In my office in Japan, I, too, took a broad approach. Instead of hiding out and being ashamed of who I was, I opened up my home to my colleagues. I explained to them that it was very normal for me to have people over to my apartment. I showed them pictures of my home, my family, and my friends. And although I was still an outsider, once I had opened up and revealed myself more fully, they knew my story and now I was less of a curiosity.

Make similarities stronger than your differences

Now let's move on to look at some other issues that can stop you in your tracks.

There are four common barriers to success:
1. Barrier 1: The pros must outweigh the cons.
2. Barrier 2: People can be suspicious of change.
3. Barrier 3: Show me the money.
4. Barrier 4: Different, or a little different?

Barrier 1: The pros must outweigh the cons.

I once worked with a guy who was well known as a jerk—a brilliant guy—but still a jerk who was demanding, manipulative, and generally not a very nice person. He always seemed to like to rub people the wrong way and almost prided himself on that. He made more enemies than friends. His personality issues were tolerated because he could offer something unique and different: great ideas and new business development abilities. When the company was doing well, and he was bringing in new clients, he could do no wrong.

And so he was tolerated…until his team began to lose business. Then people began to notice his rude attitude more than his great ideas, his difficult ways more than his brilliant schemes, and his poor relationship skills rather than the high-paying clients he had brought in but who had now grown tired of him and had left.

He had made few friends at the company, so he had few supporters, and no one who would go to bat for him when he was asked to leave. Someone who was less creative, but was much less of a jerk, was brought in to replace him.

Barrier 2: People can be suspicious of change.

Although people like things that are different, they may also panic when they encounter the unknown. Your boss may have this kind of conversation going on inside his or her heads: "This chump wants to do things differently and we don't know if that will work. This could make me look really dumb and I could lose my job. I need to put the brakes on, before I lose my corner office and end up in the mailroom." So the boss may smile sweetly and say no to your wise but wacky idea.

How can you make sure that your boss (or the decision maker if you're working with a client) will not squash the idea, or try to compromise, but instead will bite the bullet? How can you overcome this resistance, this barrier?

It's important to see the personal impact of doing something different on the decision-maker. Communication is the key. Be sure that you
constantly stress the benefits of doing this differently. Ask questions to
find out what, if anything, is bothering people and be ready to compromise on selected details if that will keep the project or idea alive.

Barrier 3: Show me the money.

Even though we may see the value of a project that we champion,
the boss or client may not want to pay for that value. There are a number
of options for the boss or the client who does not get how this investment will work out: They can abandon the idea, they can try to get the
price reduced or more likely get you to change your vision to something
less different and more conservative.

For example, a corporation wants to make a promotional video, but
is nervous the video might go wrong. The corporation decides not to go
with the wacky promo company, who has a surfboard in the reception
area, even though its proposal was imaginative and interesting. Instead,
an internal department that normally does the photos for identity badges
takes on the project. The department comes up with a conservative idea
that makes everyone feel comfortable. But the managers are still not
sure so they look at how they can make sure the video doesn't cost
much. Then if it goes wrong they won't have to worry about justifying
the expense.

The company now looks for places to cut money in the production.
Instead of using professional actors, they use John in accounting, who
does magic for kid's parties, Maureen from HR, who starred in her high
school theater class play her senior year in 2002, and Jorge, who did a
really nice job taking pictures of his niece's birthday party.

The rationale for cutting costs was that if the video goes wrong, then
the company doesn't lose too much money. It's a poor rationale, because
amateur actors are unlikely to pull off a video that the company will be
proud of. In the long term, it is more costly due to the lost opportunity
costs and project credibility. With the conservative idea and the lack of
money, the result is unlikely to be a success.

People are risk adverse. So you need to point out carefully the risks
of both going with an outsider and going with an insider solution. Be

ready to make the case in language that the employer or client understands—whether it's data, statistics, or colorful stories.

Barrier 4: Different, or a little different?

Breaking the mold is difficult. Advertising and marketing experts spend all day trying to come up with something different. As the world changes so, too, does what constitutes "different." In the medieval times in England, when travel was rare, an exotic animal such as an elephant was unusual and different. Only a few lucky people would have even seen a picture of one. In the 21st century with global communication and pop culture the elephant is seen everywhere in the media and you can go to your local zoo to see one in the flesh.

Some outsiders get stuck in a cliché. They were different at one point but they didn't notice that around them things were changing too. What was unusual 10 or 20 years ago is now common.

But sometimes some outsiders are too different. They forget that they have to work with insiders. They don't connect with insiders. They end up without work, unhappy, and unfulfilled. There are five factors that you need to consider to avoid issues about getting careers where you are an outsider on the inside.

- Factor 1: Successful outsiders realize the power of infrastructure.
- Factor 2: Successful outsiders live in the present but remember the past.
- Factor 3: Successful outsiders do not create worlds that are closed.
- Factor 4: Successful outsiders do not avoid the world.
- Factor 5: Successful outsiders do not live on an island.

Factor 1. Successful outsiders realize the power of infrastructure.

Andy Warhol was a successful outsider who made a fortune selling art. In his early days in Pittsburgh, he started work drawing illustrations and designing layouts for advertising. Maybe it's not a coincidence that one of the most commercially successful artists in his own lifetime had a beginning where he had to think about both art *and* business. This foundation in the profit and loss world of business gave him a unique perspective on art. He understood the power of the gallery system. He knew the importance of wealthy patrons. He knew the impact of being seen in the right places with the right people. The bottom line was that he understood business and marketing.

He was an outsider in his art, but in his business sense he was a total insider. He knew that without an infrastructure and organization working for him, he would likely never make any money as an artist.

If he had worked in a studio, on in an artists' colony small town on one of the remote Florida Keys, never meeting anybody apart from other artists and never developing relationships with galleries he could easily have died in obscurity. Instead, he chose to create The Factory, a working environment in the middle of New York, which was full of people assisting him in all kinds of ways. It was, as the name suggests, a place where he manufactured his work to be sold.

Unless we want to make a deliberate choice for isolation or insulation, we cannot be so different, or so idealistic, that we overlook that we live and work in a world driven by supply and demand, dollars and cents—or we risk not reaching our fullest potential.

Factor 2. Successful outsiders live in the present but remember the past.

In the first factor we need to remember to work within a structure. Often these structures are already established, sometimes for many years. If we are different we can ignore or try to change the infrastructure but that may be hard going. Instead we may want to recognize that there were reasons that things were created in the past and accept that we have to work within them. We do live in the present but if we ignore the past we may make our lives harder than necessary.

In times of change, companies often introduce new ideas as if they will cure all ills. The assumption is that what was there was junk and needs to be replaced. And that this new idea, project, or plan will make everything okay. Even if that is true, which it rarely is, it makes everyone upset. They have been happily working, plugging away in the organization, and now somebody tells them what they created is worthless.

When Coke introduced New Coke, it was forgotten that for years customers had been very happy with the product. Why did it need to be changed? What was wrong with the old Coke? New Coke failed as a concept because there was not enough attention paid to a highly successful legacy product. It did, however, give Coca Cola a powerful lesson in brand loyalty. In 1995 at a special employee event, then Chairman and Chief Executive Officer Roberto Goizueta explained the misstep about New Coke, which was a clear case of not honoring the past.

We set out to change the dynamics of sugar colas in the United States, and we did exactly that—albeit not in the way we had planned.
—www.thecoca-colacompany.com/heritage/cokelore_newcoke.html

As an outsider, you can be much more successful building on and respecting value already built than creating something completely new.

Factor 3. Successful outsiders do not create worlds that are closed.

If we are going to be successful we need customers. I have friends who don't fit in at their work and spend a lot of their free time on their true passion. One woman is a lawyer, but also an accomplished artist. She is known in her office as slightly off the wall. She wears unlawyer-like clothes—too colorful, loud, and wild. She works hard but never receives the true rewards she deserves. She hasn't been made partner and works more hours than most of her coworkers. Her job is a constant struggle.

For fun, she designs and paints her own holiday cards, which everyone loves. Her friends have asked to buy them but she doesn't want to sell them. She sticks with her job, never tells anybody at her work about her talent, and will not share it with anyone. She could be a success in the field of art. But she has chosen to be just an outsider. Her art is good—as good as art, which is sold out in the real world. She loves doing that work but through fear she hangs on to her job as a lawyer trying to persuade herself that she is fine at the job or telling herself that she will follow her passion soon. But soon never comes. One of her issues is that she doesn't share her hobby so she has no chance of selling her work or making a business through contacts. If we would be open then she might be able to go from a hobby to a small business to something that could support her. She will never know while she does her painting in secret.

Factor 4: Successful outsiders do not avoid the world.

We should create a world that is open to other people who are different from us. The person who always gets top grades at school creates a large group of admiring teachers and family, but only a small group of peers as friends. Often to get these grades, the person must miss out on social opportunities and all kinds of spontaneous fun.

Other people hide out in knowledge. They know everything there is to know about wireless technology, baseball, or quilting. People are impressed, but only a limited number of people want to talk about that knowledge.

If you are going to take your success to higher levels—professionally, commercially, and financially—you have to do market research, develop business plans, strategies and interact with customers. This doesn't mean that you have to cold-call yourself into a stupor but it does mean that you cannot stay at home and talk only to your cat.

I won the opportunity to script 13 different video programs for one company only because, when talking to my client at lunch, I mentioned that I had previously worked for a company where I had written scripts. This fact wasn't relevant to what I was talking about. I wasn't trying to sell myself. I was simply interacting, but my client remembered this nugget of information and put me on the project. If I had avoided talking to her, avoided having lunch, avoided sharing information with her, I would have missed a grand opportunity and been stuck twiddling my thumbs.

Factor 5: Successful outsiders do not live on an island.

It can be lonely being different. When I worked freelance, I created a world where I could work for a company but not get involved with the boring administration: time reporting, appraisals, and team rah-rah meetings.

It was perfect. I could do the job I liked doing and ignore the administration which at the time I didn't like. I created a world that suited my personality. I had an office but I came in when it suited me. I didn't work with any particular teams but did my own thing. At first I was lonely. I didn't have support. I didn't have the camaraderie of working together with a group of people. I was the freelancer who came in every now and then. I realized that I had to be with people. I connected with a group of other freelancers, threw a monthly lunch, and connected with e-mail and phone calls, so I had support and friendship.

We have looked at when you can be too different to be successful. Now is there ever a danger of not being different enough?

The answer is yes.

A friend of mine, who works for a producer for a television network, would stand out in a conventional corporate environment. She wears trendy but very casual clothes, has traveled and lived all over the world, has come up with many cutting-edge ideas for programs, and is known for being an outsider.

But her outsider title is slipping. In her part of the entertainment world she is not unusual. None of her colleagues wear business suits, everyone has backpacked around Nepal, and most of them have produced cutting-edge programs. She found herself getting stale, not coming up with new ideas, and getting stuck in her own style. She almost lost her job to her assistant who was a wild and wacky, was a lot younger (and therefore could be paid less), could eat fire at company parties (okay, that's an exaggeration, but she was definitely talented), and was coming up with new ideas and interesting programming.

Suddenly my friend realized she was not an outsider anymore. She was an insider and her assistant was an outsider. She began to learn about new technologies she had resisted. She met new and different talent to get interesting ideas. And she changed her image and took up new hobbies, including belly dancing. Now she is back to being a successful outsider.

The point is that if we slip from outsider to insider we lose our unique selling proposition. If we fit in too well, we can find ourselves being run of the mill.

Be Inspired to Keep Going

We may doubt who we are. We may let fear stop us. We may accept being an unsuccessful outsider if the going gets tough. We may even give up, but if we give up we have no chance of success. While we keep trying we have a possibility of success. When we give up we have nothing. It's worth fighting for. One thing we can do is look to those who blazed these trails before us and be inspired by their courage and success.

Lucille Ball is one of those archetypal characters of the 20th century. The red-headed star of a long-running television series, she was also a successful businesswoman running her own studio. That alone made her an outsider. She took on the Hollywood machine and created her own ways of producing television and doing business with her company Desilu (Desi Arnaz and Lucille Ball). But she was also an outsider in other ways. She was married to a Cuban with a Cuban accent. This was the era of white America when everyone on the screen was white, and the few who were not were doing secondary roles (to put it politely, servants and crooks, more accurately). Lucy and Desi were the stars of the show so this was a breakthrough. She also became pregnant. Up until this point, Hollywood perpetuated the stork theory of human reproduction. No one was shown pregnant on screen and kids were seen (from a polite distance) and not heard. Lucy was actually pregnant on the show, and her newborn son was part of the storyline and became a character on the show.

She always makes me laugh, and she inspires me to think how far she went in becoming a successful outsider. If she is one of your heroes too, then remember her when the chips are down.

More recent mavericks include Teddy Roosevelt, FDR, JFK, and Steve Jobs. Steve Jobs who dropped out of college, became a Buddhist, and founded Apple.

Consider another celebrity, politician, or figure you respect and admire and use them for inspiration—there is no shortage on information, and inspirational stories are widely accessible on the Internet.

Sometimes we need to remind ourselves that we are not alone. When we face barriers, knowing this can be inspirational, motivating, and comforting.

Becoming a Long-Term Successful Outsider

How will you keep on being successful as an outsider? How do we make doing the right thing a habit? And finally, how can you continue to turn your unique passions into benefits and valuable selling points?

Maintaining success in the long term is about making this new way of being at work a habit and a part of your normal behavior. An effective way of looking at how you create a habit and engrain it in your being is to focus on four levels or areas:

1. The Physical: What are we doing to be a successful insider?
2. The Mental: How our thoughts can affect our career.
3. The Emotional: Managing our feelings about being an outsider.
4. The Spiritual: How do we relate to our purpose in life?

Each level interacts with the others. For example, we may be stressed. That's on the emotional level. It will manifest on the physical level as a stomach ulcer.

We'll look at each area and suggest ways of becoming more effective.

The Physical

What can you be doing on the physical level to make sure that you remain a success as an outsider on the inside? What concrete actions can you take that help you remain in the career that works for you? What tasks should you set yourself to complete? For me it comes down to these key actions:

1. Setting an Intention
2. Creating a Vision and Mission Statements
3. Developing an Action Plan
4. Measuring Success
5. Utilizing a Support Team

1. Setting an intention

Setting an intention is vital for maintaining success. An intention is having a purpose in mind. Sometimes intention is confused with goal. An intention is different to a goal. When I set a goal to get a job in finance paying $100,000 I have specific needs for a particular job. For example, I need to be a portfolio manager. When I set an intention to find work that is financially rewarding and intellectually motivating I have specific parameters but I am open to what kind of work I do. My intention could be met if I become a portfolio manager or a lawyer or a curator. A goal relies on us doing all the work. An intention ties to the power of the universe. We work hard at our goals without help. We ask for help from a higher power than us when we set an intention.

2. Creating a vision and mission statements

We can build on our intention by modeling ourselves on effective companies. Successful organizations start by establishing a vision and mission statement. A vision statement is where the company sees itself in the future. A mission statement includes what the company does and why it is in business.

My vision is to "work globally"—I want to spend time in different parts of the world doing my work. My mission statement is, "To educate and entertain in the world"—this is more specific on what I do. It gives me a direction to follow and a clear focus. The "entertain" part of my mission statement is the outsider part of my personality. Most training and coaching is not about entertaining but purely about educating. What makes me special is that I combine both. I work with many clients from the entertainment industry. I love to have fun, bring a playful attitude, and use humor in my work. I also write plays and scripts that entertain, but often educate as well. The "in the world" part of my mission statement signifies that I work globally. I have clients around the world and have worked in Asia, Europe, and the United States. My mission sums me up perfectly, but, more importantly, it provides me with direction—like a compass needle pointing north and guiding toward the highest expression of my gifts and outsider uniqueness.

3. Developing an action plan

From my mission, I then created an action plan. My plan contains goals, tasks, and steps. I decide on the resources I need: my schedule and my budget. You need an action plan for your career, which contains you career goals (this year, in five years, and in 10 years, and how you will get there). In Chapter 12 you will get to put together an action plan based on what you have learned in this book.

4. Measuring success

In your plan you should have measures of success. Those could include not only the final prize of getting a job but also metrics that you need to meet on the way. For example, how many people did I talk to today? How many applications did I make? How many interviews did I go on?

The metrics enable you to measure how well you are doing, or alert you if you are veering off course, getting lazy, or losing sight of your goals. Your metrics help you to answer these questions: "Am I hitting my deadlines? Reaching my goals? Doing what I said I would be doing?"

This principle applies when looking for work or new clients. You may think you have not made many phone calls, so you need to quantify what constitutes a reasonable number of calls. Set a goal—five or 50 calls a day, for example, depending on your situation and goals—so that you can measure your success against this metric. If you're not meeting the goal, either the goal is not realistic or you have a barrier getting in the way. If you are not sure which, consult with a friend, colleague, or coach who understands your career goals.

You need to keep records of how many contacts you made, how many jobs you applied for, and how many interviews you had. Good salespeople know that the more calls they make, the nearer they are to making a sale. Finding a job or getting freelance work is a numbers game, same as sales.

5. Utilizing a support team

When actors get an Oscar they often end up listing name after name in their acceptance speech. *Who are all these people,* you may ask. I would answer that they are the celebrity's support team. The agent, publicist, manager, make-up person, and wardrobe person all need to be on the actor's team.

Your support team might include a coach, a lawyer, a mentor, a friend who will be honest with you, and even your mom! It can really help to have someone who will tell you the truth or who will open up your eyes.

It can work to have someone hold you accountable to complete certain tasks. Sometimes I use a coach, mentor, or friend to support me with my tasks. Sometimes I create a deadline that helps me focus on completion.

Now that we have looked at the physical level we can go to the next level, the mental level.

The Mental

- Head Versus Heart
- Valid but Not True
- Limiting Beliefs
- Being in the Flow
- Affirmations

The mental level is all about our thoughts; what are we thinking and how is that affecting what we are doing in our careers and in our goals. The power of thought is well known in every field from healthcare—

where it has been shown that those patients who think about positive outcomes to their illnesses are more like to recover and to do it faster than those who focus on the negative—through to sports, where sports psychology is a huge business helping men and women think about wining results. In becoming a long-term success we must take our mental level into account.

1. Head versus heart

The battle between the head and the heart is an old one. For years we have been told to follow our hearts while at the same time being reminded to use our heads! No wonder we are confused.

Thinking can come from the head or the heart. The thinking that we do from our head is often faulty and may not be in our best interests. It can be based on other people's thoughts, or on incomplete information, or on biases or prejudices. The thinking that we do from our heart is always in line with what is true to us.

Our head thinking relates to our fears about ourselves and other people. It tells us what to do, but the information is often only based on part of the story. It orders us to "relax," "focus on the money," and "get through it." It's not the worst advice but this information is not complete. We might hate the work so much that it makes us sick.

Our heart might be telling us something different. It will be looking at the big picture, at the whole situation, not just this one incident. Our heart might be saying, "be calm," "be open to learning about this situation," and "explore other possibilities." It will be reflecting our deeper truth and values.

When we go for an interview and our head is telling us that this is a great job and yet our heart is warning that this is a great job but it means lots of stress because of travel, long hours, and a demanding work environment, we are foolish if we ignore our intuition. If we go with our head, we will make the money, but we will not be happy or fulfilled. The more you can tap into your heart the smoother your journey from unsuccessful outsider to successful outsider will be.

2. Valid but not true

An important distinction I make with all my clients who are job hunting or changing careers is the one between what is valid and true.

Many of my clients will talk about their dream job and almost immediately talk about why they couldn't go for it, why it's impossible to try, and end up with a statement like this: "Everyone I talk to says this is a bad idea."

That's valid. That really is. But it's not true. By that I mean lots of people, if not all people would agree. But does that mean that it's not possible? No. Anything as we have seen time and time again, even from recent history is possible—men walking on the moon, an African-American U.S. president, smoking being banned in France.

So you want to write a screenplay, or start a landscaping garden business, or give up work and stay home with your children. If you ask people, especially people you choose, they will all support you, notion that this is difficult, not a wise move, or even dumb. Yet I have clients who write screenplays, who have started landscape gardening businesses, and who have given up work to stay home with their children.

In your career journey, especially as an outsider, you will be told to believe what the majority tells you. Choose whether you do by looking in your heart and seeing what is true for you. Go for the truth. It may not be easy, or straightforward, or successful immediately, but it will be part of your learning about yourself and your work life.

3. Limiting beliefs

Just as the opinion of everyone masquerading as the truth can stop you so can limiting beliefs. A belief is something that we hold as true, which guides the way we do things in our lives. For example, I believe in people being treated fairly. That's a belief that will influence what I do and say—so I may stand up for a person who is being treated unfairly or support causes in which I believe fairness is an issue. A limiting belief is a belief that we think is true and also guides the way we do things in our lives. For example, a limiting belief that I used to have was that my work was good but not quite good enough. This influenced what I did and said.

So for example, when I first started work on this book, I spent a lot of time writing and rewriting it. I got lots of praise, got close to publishing, but it seemed like something always got in the way. Then through coaching and counseling, I found out that I had a limiting belief around the book's success. I realized that I thought the book was good but not good enough. Once I identified this, and did some healing work around the belief, the fortune of the book turned around. Within less than three months, I had created a new proposal, secured a great agent, and got this publisher. Until I had done some inner work with a coach and counselor, I did not even know I had a limiting belief. My limiting belief was replaced with the new belief that my work was good and that I wanted to share it with the world.

Your limiting belief may be, "I can't go back to college, I'm too old," or "I'm no good with numbers," or just that "I'm not cut out for my own business." This is a fundamental lesson for becoming a long-term success—identify the limiting belief, work on it with professional help, and turn it around to something more supportive of your future.

4. Being in the flow

Being in the flow means that you actually stop thinking and trying to work out in your head what to do about your work situation. Instead you give up on the analysis, worry, and anxiety, and hand over the issue to your heart. Instead of thinking everything through, and trying to control things in your life, you allow things to happen. Not just randomly but as part of a bigger picture and plan.

So for example, you can go to a networking event, and when you get there find it has been canceled. Using your head you will probably end up getting angry, frustrated, upset, and more, because your mind will be telling you that you have wasted your time, and the purpose of the event—networking and getting offered a job—did not work out. Your head may even start blaming you for not checking to see if it was still on, telling you that you shouldn't have signed up in the first place, and even berating you for the situation, saying that this is typical of the way you manage your affairs—badly. It is quite possible that your head blames some of this on you being an outsider. Your head would probably remind you that an insider would not get themselves into such a mess.

But if you were to allow yourself to be in the flow, letting your heart and intuition guide you, you might have a different experience. You might notice a great coffee shop right by the networking event, with free parking, music, and home-made cookies. You could decide to get a cup of java to kill time while you wait for the traffic to die down. You could really enjoy the place, start talking to the couple at the next table, and find yourself having dinner with them at a great Cuban place nearby.

They could turn out to be recruiters for a new company. They are looking for people just like you. They love the fact that you are different and they especially love the fact that you did not get upset by the cancellation of the event but went with the flow. The end result could be a perfect evening of networking with a job offer. Your primary goal would be met.

It can be tough to go with the flow. It is one of those over-used phrases that can often sound trite, but when you step back it is still a powerful statement. *Go with the flow* means follow your heart. Following your heart will be much more successful than letting your head rule your life.

5. Affirmations

Affirmations are positive statements such as "I am supported by a great team" or "I have everything I need to be a success in business" or "I am following my heart." Affirmations help to turn around negative thinking or thoughts. If we have a limiting belief, or we are scared of doing something, or we are not sure what to do next and are confused, we can use positive affirmations to turn around those negative thoughts and get back on the right career and work track.

The most effective affirmations are those that are not driven by your ego and your head. Affirmations such as "I am richer than everyone I know" or "I beat all the competition, whatever the cost" or "I am skinny like a super model" may be effective but they do not come from your heart and are not aligned with your own personal truth.

More effective affirmations are those that are not just about us or do not put ourselves up above other people. So affirmations such as "I am living in abundance" or "I am always playing to win" or "I am in perfect health and fitness" are better. Those affirmations do not tie you to specific goals that may not be connected to who you are.

Affirmations are used by actors and athletes and sales people and soldiers, and there are many books that talk more about creating affirmations and how to use them. Use affirmations to help you move to being a successful outsider in the long term.

The Emotional

The emotional level is about how we feel and how those feelings impact how we behave. It is hard to be successful finding a job, changing careers, or becoming a successful insider if we are feeling down, depressed, or desperate. To keep on being successful we need to be able to look at those feelings, acknowledge them, and work through them. It makes sense to look at what is going on when you are feeling upset or anxious.

The Emotional level is about:

1. Fear
2. Anger
3. Doubt
4. Blame
5. Contentment

1. Fear

Fear is the biggest emotion that takes the outsider off course. We fear because we believe we are not good enough and don't measure up to other people. Or we fear failure, or even success. Fear is at the bottom of many of our negative emotions.

2. Anger

Anger is often shielding a fear. We feel angry with the healthcare system because we are afraid of getting sick and not being taken care of or not being able to pay for treatment; we are angry with our spouse because we are afraid we made the wrong choice or that he or she will leave us or will stay with us in an abusive relationship; and we are angry with ourselves for not getting that degree or MBA, and we are afraid that we may have left it too late and that we will never be successful or able to pay the bills or whatever runs around our head.

When we get angry with something or someone we need to look at what we are angry within inside.

3. Doubt

Often when my clients are expressing doubt it is because they are focused on the past rather than the future. What do I mean by that? I mean that they are not open to changing careers or finding a new job because when they tried that before it didn't work out.

For example, a client applied to grad school in his 20s and was turned down. Now he is in his 30s with lots of experience, but he still believes that, if he tries for grad school he will get rejected, so he doubts whether he should even try or is pessimistic about his chances of being successful.

How can we handle this? By deciding that the past is the past and the present is the present. Although we can repeat our mistakes from the past, we don't have to. We can choose to focus on what went wrong or we can look to the future and see what can go wrong.

4. Blame

We are often discouraged and feel like giving up on career plans or work ideas. We are moving along and then we stop because of something external to us. Often we stop because of what other people have to say. We listen to their opinions and let them influence us. When we blame people because something in our plan goes wrong or we don't get the result we expected we are also focusing on the external.

Many of us believe that it is easier to let other people drive us off track or blame them when it goes wrong rather than owning up to our responsibility and accountability. We are trained and educated in our world to look for reasons why things don't work out, and it is simple to find someone or something as a reason for the misstep or downfall.

What is much harder is to look at what we bring to the issue and see why we are discouraged or blaming others. Usually the answer lies in ourselves. We are letting others influence us or we blame others because we do not believe in ourselves. If we are confident in who we are then we don't need to get blown off course by opinions and we don't need to blame when things don't go our way; we can simply learn from the issue.

5. Contentment

Contentment can be a very positive state, needing nothing, and living in peace. But it can also mean we are settling. The job is not exactly what we job hunters want, yet we don't feel confident enough to move forward with anything different.

We can be content with our pay, working conditions, and job responsibilities, but we can still be bored with our job. If we are bored or content with our work we are missing out on a chance to help us connect. We are not seeing how our part helps the bigger goals.

The Spiritual

For many people, talk of the spiritual can be challenging. It either conjures up a picture of religion (and a particular religion at that, being Catholic,

Buddhist, Jewish, etc.) or self-help, and then a particular expert or theory in that field (Oprah, Tony Robbins, The Secret). Outsiders have been marginalized by religions or philosophies. So it is understandable to be nervous.

The Spiritual level areas are:
1. Connecting to a Higher Power
2. Being a Spiritual Being
3. Measuring Time
4. Living in Abundance

1. Connecting to a higher power

Connecting to a higher power means that you have a team on your side. When your career is not going as you planned or you hit a road block, instead of working it out on your own, you have the choice of working with your team. This team understands you, is objective, supports you, and wants the best for you.

How do you connect? Prayer is a traditional means but it does not need to look traditional. Prayer can mean kneeling in a 12th-century church and asking God for guidance or standing in a circle at the beach and thanking Mother Nature for her wonders. If the word *prayer* doesn't work then think of it as a conversation. Having a conversation with your inner guide can be very helpful. Connecting with a higher power or your inner guide enables you get help as you work through your career issues.

2. Being a spiritual being

Another concept I have found very useful is that we are souls or spiritual beings or sources of energy in a body or living as humans. The concept here is that at our core we all share a truth about ourselves, other people, and the world. This core truth connects to our heart. We can access this truth through our intuition. Truth is perfect and complete. On the outside is our body, the human part of us. This is connected to our head. It is imperfect and incomplete.

What does this mean for us? It means that we will often stumble because being human is about making mistakes (and learning from our errors), but if we look inside we will always find answers.

So when you start your own business and then find yourself with a fine because you forgot to get a license from the city, you can chalk that up to being human. You can learn from this incident but you don't have to beat yourself up. The inner spirit or energy knows that you are doing your best and that your business is going to help other people and is part of your career journey. You took a wrong step but the path is still right.

This is especially important for outsiders, who are often hard on themselves for doing something different. This concept gives permission not to have everything done perfectly or completely. Of course this can also scare some of us. What? It doesn't have to be done perfectly? It doesn't have to be complete? No, no it doesn't. And actually it never will be. Because we are working on a human level. But will it be true? Yes, indeed. And will it help our careers? I believe so. And serve our journey to being successful outsiders? Certainly!

The concept is like going on a journey and breaking down on the way, or taking a detour because of construction or faulty map-reading, or having to stop and take a job washing dishes, because you run out of money, BUT still getting to your destination. The truth will be a compass to keep you heading in the right direction.

3. Measuring time

Another concept that I find of great help is one concerning time. We just talked about going on a journey and how even if we get delayed the destination stays the same. But we may worry that we are taking too long, that the stops and starts are preventing us from reaching our goals. In the 21st century we spend a lot of time worrying about not being able to finish things. We are worried that we will fail. We are sure that if we don't do something, something even worse will happen. Or if we are not on time we will miss out and that will be our last chance.

As outsiders those feelings are even stronger. We have faced challenges for being different so we often work even harder to make up for that.

I wanted to go to Oxford University but I did not get high enough grades. That opportunity seems to be over. Although I know that anything is possible, I see that my time for that adventure has gone. And it makes me sad (just a little).

It makes me sad because of the belief that there was *one* chance and I blew it. If we look at time as fixed, then that's true. If we look at time as more fluid, we don't know. I don't know if maybe I get another shot in another lifetime to go to Oxford. Or maybe I don't need to worry because it's already happened in a previous lifetime. You may not believe in other lives. That's fine. I don't know either, but what I do know is that believing that I only had one shot is much harder to accept that the possibility that I have another chance at a dream.

If we look at time not as a fixed period but as a continuous event suddenly we don't have to worry so much about getting things done, being on time, and having everything complete. When we relax about these things, our head thoughts stop and we have time to listen to our heart more. We may even find that our heart is telling us that the things we thought were so important to finish really aren't.

4. Living in abundance

The bottom line is that we all want to be living in abundance in the long term. What does that mean? It means that resources are there for us. We often think that means money, but money is only one piece of the pie. You can be the richest person in the world and not have an abundance of time, peace, or love in your life.

As an outsider on a career path how do you find an abundance of jobs, work opportunities, or new clients if you have your own business? There is no easy answer to that, but there are a series of steps you can take that will help you with creating a world of abundance.

Be open to the idea of abundance. If you can't believe that abundance is possible then you won't be able to enjoy it. If you have lots of stories why you can't get more money at your job, or more customers, or more peace, then your first step is to look at those limiting beliefs and turn them around to ones that support you.

Create a vision of abundance. What does abundance look like for you? Time to spend in your boat on the weekends? Money for your retirement? Lots of interviews for the next job? For everyone it will mean different things. It helps to describe what abundance looks like for you.

You can do that in different ways. You can write out a description of everything abundance means to you. Use the present tense so you are describing it as happening now, not in the future. Be detailed in your description. And make sure you describe it not just from your head thoughts but also from your heart. Or you can create a picture either as a drawing or a collection of pictures and words that you collect and make into a scrapbook project.

Keep affirming that vision. Once you have the vision of abundance it's good to read the description or look at the picture regularly. This could be every day or every week or even monthly. But the more often the better. You are looking to change your view of what abundance looks like so the more you are seeing a different view the better.

As an outsider, you really want to be consistent in this. So often being different is brought up to you that it can take you off balance. If your vision includes being healthy and having lots of energy for your new business, but then when you get criticized for your ideas by your family you reach for the cookies, you need to keep going back to the vision. This will help you get over those bumps in the road.

Work on barriers to abundance. If you are finding that abundance is still eluding you, you need to see if any barriers are coming up for you and what they are.

We have looked at limiting beliefs—those can be reasons why you don't find abundance occurring. Work through those limiting beliefs if that is the case.

Or use your inner guide to discuss what is happening. Maybe your vision of abundance doesn't serve you. You are asking for a high-powered job making six figures but you have not thought what that will mean for you in terms of job satisfaction.

Whatever you do, don't give up on living in abundance. Remember you are on a journey; the destination is the same, even if you have a flat tire or the cops pull you over!

Celebrate your successes. If you have success in creating abundance, celebrate it. Give yourself a pat on the back. Treat yourself to a fattening treat. Or tell your friends what's happened. And be grateful. Thank yourself for your hard work. Thank your friends and family for being there for you. Thank the higher power or your inner guide if that feels comfortable.

About 12 years ago, I went through the process I've described to create abundance. I created a vision by writing down what I wanted abundance to look like. I described having interesting and well-paid work, a comfortable home with a pool, a long-term and committed relationship and a family and that I would be driving a white Mercedes that was paid for! Soon after creating this I met my partner (of 12 years and counting and we have a 4-year-old son). We have a comfortable and welcoming home with a pool (which we actually rent out). But the strangest part of this abundance exercise was that I forgot all about the car request until I was driving one day. I looked around me and realized that my white Mercedes—which was paid for—was actually a manifestation of what I had imagined years before. Abundance is possible.

12
PUTTING IT ALL TOGETHER

In this chapter, we will take all of the outsider insights, tools, and strategies that you've learned, and put it all together to create a highly personalized career game plan, or blueprint. To do so, you have a choice of either—or both—of two options, each of which will reinforce the book's knowledge and wisdom to integrate it fully into your life for a profoundly positive and lasting impact.

Option One: Action Plan

With Option One, you have an outline for creating an Action Plan that you can use to develop goals and tasks, and implementing specific steps to build momentum and achieve measurable progress. It includes a system for monitoring and charting your progress, to keep you solidly on course to reach your greatest goals for outsider success.

Option Two: Personalized Approach

The Personalized Approach gives you an opportunity to express yourself in more creative, less structured ways. Proven techniques include journaling, creating a vision board, developing an outside/inside journey that plots both the spiritual and practical steps necessary, and other innovative techniques such as free-form writing, theater games, and found-object art.

Either the Action Plan or the Personalized Approach can be used by you alone or with a group.

Action Plans

The whole reason to have an Action Plan is to research and reflect your options before you jump in. Spending time on paper is much better than spending your savings, or, worse, your family's or friend's cash, on a business or a career change that fails. Fail in the planning and chances are that you will fail in the endeavor too. Succeed in the planning and your chances of being a successful outsider go up exponentially.

Initially, we'll follow the fictional example of John to help us understand the Action Plan process. John is a creative video producer who works internally in a large oil and gas corporation. Mostly, he records executives making presentations that are to be distributed to other employees around the country. They are dull speeches, and he's not.

We'll start with Phase 1: Assessing who you are. John will be answering these questions based on the ideas in this book.

Phase 1: Who are you?

1.1. How Are You an Outsider? – Your Current Status

Which of the Five Stand-Out Signifiers apply to you?

1. Outsiders look different.
2. Outsiders sound different.
3. Outsiders act different.
4. Outsiders feel different.
5. Outsiders are made to feel different.

John's Answer

I guess that I feel different, #4. I am interested in movies and the movie business. Nobody at work seems to care about that much. I don't seem to connect with other people.

1.2 Your Outsider Story

Describe how this makes you feel right now. What is your story about how you feel as an outsider at work?

John's Answer

I always want to do something more creative at work but my bosses don't. They criticize, dismiss, belittle my best ideas, and that makes me feel like I'm not good at what I do. I get depressed at the thought of going to work.

1.3 Your Future Status: What Is Your Vision?

Talk about what is important to you in your work life. This is not the time to get specific, but rather this is the time to go to your heart. It provides the framework for how you go forward.

John's Answer

I want to have fun, be respected, and be appreciated.

1.4 Your Future Status: What Is Your Mission?

Now you can get more specific. This is when you talk about what you want to do based upon your outsider qualities.

John's Answer

I want to be making videos that strongly impact or move the people that see them. I want to make videos that people will say wow, *videos that they will remember, think about, and talk about afterward, videos that can be submitted for industry awards. I want videos that make people think and laugh too!*

1.5 Your Future Status: Values

What do you value most in who you are, and in the kind of work you do? These form the foundation for how you live your life, what you stand for, why you get up in the morning.

John's Answer
Quality
Creativity
Integrity
Educating Others
Respecting Others

1.6 Your Future Status: What Are Your Benchmarks for Success?

How will you know you have become a successful outsider at work? What one thing would tell you, both in your heart and in your head?

John's Answer

I'll want to get up on Monday mornings eager and looking forward to go to work!

1.7 Your Future Status: What Is Your Personal Commitment?

Now how do you feel about this plan? Any change you feel in yourself? You might be frightened. You could be excited. You might be feeling that and more. But how committed are you? It's okay to have some doubts, but you'll need to commit to try, to keep going even when it is difficult!

John's Answer

This is putting into words what I've been feeling for a long time, and now it seems a whole lot clearer to me. That is, I've been working this job for four years and I really think I deserve better. I'm ready and committed.

1.8 Your Future Status: What Are Your Personal Barriers?

There may be barriers to you becoming a successful outsider. List those here. For example, for many people money may well be an issue. Or finding another job. Or telling your family about your plans. It's okay to encounter barriers, but it's important to identify them so you can deal with them.

John's Answer

I'm worried about paying my bills. I can't see any other options but my job. And my dad will think I'm nuts if I tell him I am going to get a new job or go out on my own.

Now *you* can try Phase 1: Who Are You?

Phase 1: Who are you?

1.1. How Are You an Outsider? Your Current Status

Which of the Five Stand-out Signifiers apply to you, and why?

1. Outsiders look different.
2. Outsiders sound different.
3. Outsiders act different.
4. Outsiders feel different.
5. Outsiders are made to feel different.

_____

_____

_____

_____

_____

_____

_____

_____

_____

1.2 Your Outsider Story

Describe how this makes you feel right now. What is your story about how you feel as an outsider at work?

_____

_____

_____

_____

_____

_____

_____

_____

_____

1.3 Your Future Status: What Is Your Vision?

Talk about what is important to you in your work life. This is not the time to get specific, but rather this is the time to go to your heart. It provides the framework for how you go forward.

_____
_____
_____

1.4 Your Future Status: What Is Your Mission?

Now you can get more specific. This is when you talk about what you want to do based upon your outsider qualities.

_____
_____
_____

1.5 Your Future Status: Values

What do you value most in who you are, and in the kind of work you do? These form the foundation for how you live your life, what you stand for, and why you get up in the morning.

_____
_____
_____
_____
_____
_____

1.6 Your Future Status: What Are Your Benchmarks for Success?

How will you know you have become a successful outsider at work? What one thing would tell you, both in your heart and in your head?

_____
_____
_____
_____
_____
_____

1.7 Your Future Status: What Is Your Personal Commitment?

Now how do you feel about this plan? Any change you feel in yourself? You might be frightened. You could be excited. You might be feeling that and more. But how committed are you? It's okay to have some doubts, but you'll need to commit to keep going even when it is difficult!

_____

_____

_____

_____

_____

_____

1.8 Your Future Status: What Are Your Personal Barriers?

There may be some barriers to you becoming a successful outsider. List those here. For example, for many people money may well be an issue. Or finding another job. Or telling your family about your plans. It's okay to have barriers but it's important to identify them so you can deal with them.

_____

_____

_____

_____

_____

_____

Phase 2: What makes you different and how does that translate to a job or sales?

We'll continue to look at John, the corporate video producer, as an example of assessing our outsider qualities and skills for their optimal marketplace value.

2.1 What Do You Have to Offer?

Here, you want to go back to what you discovered in the earlier chapters about your unique skills. It's what makes you different, and it can be a positive or a negative, depending on the situation and our presentation.

John's Answer

I'm a great writer and I have really good ideas. I am very creative and can sometimes see connections between different things that other people don't see. But when I explain these connections, people totally get what I am saying. They say that it helps them to understand these ideas in new ways.

2.2 What Could Be Your Product or Service?

This is where you convert your skills into products or services. It's the core of this book and what we focused on in Chapter 3.

John's Answer

Writing and producing creative corporate and training videos that address boring or difficult subjects in an interesting and effective way.

For example, I had to produce a video about why we should follow company policies and procedures. I came up with a concept that showed people at an airport going on a trip under two difference scenarios. In the first scenario was an airline without procedures so everything was chaotic and confusing—no lines, no check-in process, and no set security questions. In the second scenario the airline used set procedures and the whole trip went smoothly.

2.3 Describe Your Product's or Service's Features and Benefits

A feature of some minivans is three rows of seats. For a large family, the benefit would be the extra space and roominess. Think in terms of the features of your outsider qualities, and how they become a benefit—for the right people.

John's Answer

My ability to look at subjects in a unique and unconventional way is a feature of my outsider qualities, as is my ability to see simple, clever, and clear solutions to training challenges. The benefit of this quality is that I can produce corporate or training videos that make complicated or boring subjects interesting, effective, and memorable.

Now it's your turn to complete Phase 2 for yourself.

Phase 2: What makes you different and how does that translate to a job or sales

2.1 What Do You Have to Offer?

Here, you want to go back to what you discovered in the earlier chapters about your unique skills. It's what makes you different, and it can be a positive or a negative, depending on the situation and our presentation.

_____

_____

_____

_____

_____

_____

2.2 What Could Be Your Product or Service?

This is where you convert your skills into products or services. It's the core of this book and what we focused on in Chapter 3.

_____

_____

_____

_____

_____

_____

2.3 Describe Your Product's or Service's Features and Benefits

A feature of some minivans is three rows of seats. For a large family, the benefit would be the extra space and roominess. Think in terms of the features of your outsider qualities, and how they become a benefit—for the right people.

_____

_____

_____

_____

_____

_____

Let's move on to Phase 3.

Phase 3: Selling Yourself

3.1 Marketplace and Product

First, who is your target employer, or, if you have a business, your customer? Second, how will your product or service exceed that employer's or customer's expectations?

John's Answer

I could look into training companies that make videos—or those that don't make videos but should. I have a talent that would appeal to them and produce a great product. I have some excellent samples. I think when they see that I had worked inside a large company, and took complicated concepts and made them fun and easy to understand, they will be impressed.

3.2 Pricing

How will you determine what you can earn, or what you can charge?

This is all about researching your marketplace and looking at the average salary, or the going price for your product or service. Then you can consider how your unique abilities might affect that pricing.

John's Answer

I know that the average salary for this kind of work is between $50K and $75K. I think with my background, I could ask for the top end of the range. I also believe I could bring in new business because I understand the oil and gas business. That makes me even more valuable.

3.3 Promotion

How will you brand and market yourself?

This is what you are going to do to get yourself noticed. Are you going to do the normal things—network, apply for job postings, go to job fairs? Or, are you going to be more creative and promote yourself in outsider ways?

John's Answer

I'm going to put some of my videos up on YouTube, send the link to all my friends and associates, and ask them to pass it on to all of their friends. I'm also going to compile a list of all the target companies I would work for, and see if any of my contacts know people at them. I'm also going to create a DVD with my best video samples, a video interview, and an interactive resume. I will post a profile on LinkedIn and network online to target companies and video production industry groups.

Now you can work on Phase 3 for yourself.

Phase 3: Selling yourself

3.1 Product

First, who is your target employer, or, if you have a business, your customer? Second, how will your product or service exceed that employer's or customer's expectations?

_____

_____

_____

_____

_____

3.2 Pricing

How will you determine what you can earn or what you can charge? This is all about researching your marketplace and looking at the average salary, or the going price for your product or service. Then you can consider how your unique abilities might affect that pricing.

_____

_____

_____

_____

_____

3.3 Promotion

How will you brand and market yourself?

This is what you are going to do to get yourself noticed. Are you going to do the normal things—network, apply for job postings, go to job fairs? Or, are you going to be more creative and promote yourself in outsider ways?

_____

_____

_____

_____

_____

Monitoring your plan and your success

Now you have your plan. You will want to set up a process for incorporating it into your life. One effective way is to review the information on a daily or weekly basis depending on whether you are actively seeking to make a transition. Reflect on each element, and edit or update anything that changes.

It is also important to develop and work from a set of written goals and tasks, which follow from the plan.

Goals and tasks

A goal for John might be:

Research training companies who could hire me.

That's pretty big, and could seem daunting, so you can break it down into smaller tasks that are easier to understand and to complete.

- Research training companies who could hire me.
- Go online and Google training companies in my local area?
- Select only companies that are within 25 hours of me.
- Choose only companies that produce their own videos.
- Print out the key profile information on each company.
- File it in a binder.
- Go to each target company.
- Go to the company's Website.
- Print out key pages of their services, clients, staff.
- See if they have an "employment" Webpage.
- Use LinkedIn and Plaxo to network to current and former employees and managers of target companies.

- Use Facebook or Twitter to network into these companies.
- Google the companies to look for news coverage, advertising, news releases.
- Research trade associations that may cover corporate video production.
- Look for video equipment hardware and software manufacturer trade shows video production companies may be attending; the vendors to those companies may know who is purchasing equipment and expanding.

Software options

You can do this on paper if you prefer, but there are lots of software programs that will organize the action planning process for you, especially if you like to go paperless (be sure to back up!).

Options include the very popular Franklin Covey Plan Plus, which helps you plan and decide on your priorities; VIP Organizer, which can be used for personal use and for a small business and includes action plans, reminders, and notepads; Progress Planner, available for personal and professional use with a format that allows you to plan and deal with unforeseen obstacles; CO Major Plan Plus, designed especially for students navigating their education; and RightChoiceDSS, a program that helps you make decisions more effectively based on a Wharton Business School set of techniques.

But if you don't want to buy new software don't use paper or a product you are already familiar with like Microsoft Project or Excel, go for it. If not, don't go that route unless you like learning new technology, think the investment is worthwhile, and think it will be helpful for your job or business. You may find yourself learning the program rather than learning about yourself.

Benefits of an action plan

The first benefit of an Action Plan comes with writing down the required key steps in its process. Seeing those thoughts, goals and feelings in writing gives them greater power; power that can propel you into positive action. The second benefit comes with utilizing it well throughout your lifetime, regularly reviewing and updating it—a compass needle always pointing to your true north—rather than see it as a one-off event.

Option Two: Personalized Approach

In Option Two, I will present less structured processes designed to make your vision of you—as a far more successful outsider—more concrete; a habit and a reality. Let's look at your choices.

- Journaling
- Creating a vision board
- Theater games
- Found-object art
- Something completely different

These exercises are options. You may love some, and others won't work for you. That's fine. What I want to do is give you choices.

We'll use John from our Action Plan to exemplify the value of these five powerful tools. Recall that John is a creative video producer who works for a large oil and gas corporation. He mostly records executives making presentations. They love facts and figures; he loves taking those facts and figures and converting them into images, words, action, and emotion that viewers find actionable and memorable.

Journaling

Buy a journal—it doesn't have to be hand-made from Florence, though that's nice—but it should have at least 50 to 100 pages and feel good to you. This is where you are going to record your thoughts, feelings, and actions, so it should be something you like working with.

Journal for 12 weeks. Each week you will be writing on one of the 12 chapters of this book. At the end of three months, if you have kept to the plan, you will have worked through the whole book.

Journal daily, every other day, or weekly. It helps if you do this regularly, to form a positive habit in your life. This activity is designed to support, not punish you. I find it helpful to do my journaling at the same time every day.

Journaling Pointers

Either write for a specific amount of time (assign 15 to 30 minutes), or if that doesn't work for you, set a goal of writing so many pages in a day or week.

When journaling, anything is okay. Write down whatever comes to mind. Don't stop and censor yourself. Let it flow. You may want to re-read what you wrote the day before, or it is equally fine to start a new day fresh and don't look back.

Another technique is to review your journal every month, highlight any themes you discover, and ponder them for significance or trends. Check to see if they consistent with your current goals, or are you veering off course?

John's journal entry might read like this

Frustrated with my boss today. It seems like whenever I try to do something different he squashes my ideas. It makes me feel like a little kid. That's exactly what my older brother used to do. Oh, that's interesting. I hadn't thought of that before. That feeling I get when my boss puts down one of my ideas is just like I felt when I was a kid. I wanted to please my brother so much.

I'm excited about going to meet my friend Grace for lunch tomorrow. She works on a TV show and I love the creative buzz around her. I want some of that buzz too!!!

Creating a Vision Board

A vision board is a visual representation of what's important to you and what you want to focus on and attract into your life. You can cut pictures from magazines that you love, or add words that you are drawn to from newspapers, or add your own drawings or sayings. You can add dried flowers, gold stars, or sparkly glitter. It's all your choice! Once you are finished, you display it in a place special to you.

I love doing this. It takes me back to simple times when I was at kindergarten and we worked on projects. I found it so much fun pulling all the different things together and then presenting them to my family. You may rediscover this invaluable childlike joy, all too rare in our adult lives, for yourself here.

Create a vision board for how you see yourself as a successful outsider at work. To prepare for the vision board process, collect a pile of magazines (buy them if you have to). Get poster board or flip chart paper or whatever paper you have available—select the size that works for you, and get glue, scissors, pens, glitter, and few colored marker pens. Make sure you have all that together before you launch into the project. It can be frustrating to be halfway through the process and realize you don't have scissors, glue, or the photo of a baby that is key to your concept and vision. Take as long as you want on the activity, but usually not less than an hour is a good guideline, as you want to reach beneath the surface for ideas, dreams, goals, and aspirations. Remember to have fun! When you are finished, place it in a location where you will see it often—in your office above your desk, inside a closet door so you see it as you get ready in the morning or by your front door so you see it as you come in and out. Remember to look at it regularly and to immerse yourself in the vision.

John's vision board might include a picture of his movie idols, film directors, producers, or award-winning videographers, and a paragraph from each of his favorite books. He is focused on creative writing for the screen. He might also include a picture of a classroom with happy kids in it. He loves education. He could also include a fabulous photograph he took of Niagara Falls. It is a great shot, one of his happiest moments, and it shows the power of the water. It reminds him of his creative force and motivates him to change jobs.

Theater games

I took improvisation (improv) classes at the famous Second City comedic actors' school in Chicago. It is great fun, and a surprisingly powerful way to get you out of your head and totally into the moment. As an improv student, you have to react to something as it happens, and you never know what that will be.

Theater games are usually played with a group of people. So if you are reading this book along with a group of friends or colleagues, you're all set. If you are reading this alone, then enlist some friends or family. Focus on your job or career situation.

Having fun and being in the moment is a good way of exploring the issue. If you are playing your boss and your buddies are playing you and your coworkers in the fun of the game you may well find some new feelings. This learning can be very helpful in moving your career forward.

John's game might be "Always Agree."

The aim of the game is that you agree with everything that is said. By agreeing you move the story on:

"That's a great elephant you have there."

(player mimes he has an elephant with him)

"Yes it is, I stole it from the zoo."

"Wow, me too, I stole a monkey last week, I sneaked him out under my coat."

(player mimes he has a monkey under his coat)

By disagreeing you can stop the plot from moving on:

"That's a great elephant you have there."

"I don't have an elephant."

"Oh. I thought you did."

"No."

Have a facilitator who will monitor what is being said.

The facilitator can either be you so you can observe something in your life that is causing you problems being acted out, or it can be another person, which allows you to drive the action because you are part of the issue. If you choose someone else to be the facilitator make sure that he or she is clear about the rules of the game, what you are looking for in terms of learning from the game, and what kind of notes on the process (if any) you would like.

The facilitator makes sure that everyone keeps to the rules, so if one person disagrees the facilitator stops the action and asks the person to agree.

The facilitator is also the time keeper allows between 10 and 20 minutes.

In this game, John plays himself. His friends play his boss and coworkers. John wants to look at how his work is received by his organization.

Boss (Friend 1): "Have you got that really four hour video program on how to use a stapler completed yet?"

John: "Yes I have. In fact I made it five hours and I also did one about using a hole punch. I am planning to make something about a paper clip next week."

Coworker (Friend 2): "Wow I would love to see a video about a paper clip."

John: "Me too. It's going to be the most interesting video you ever saw."

Boss (Friend 1): "It will be fascinating. Your videos are fascinating."

John: "I know. I think my best one was the 10-part series on how to fold a letter and put it in an envelope."

Coworker (Friend 2): "I loved that one."

After the exchange, John realizes that he wants his boss and co-workers to be excited about the programs he makes. But he also sees that the topics are not interesting. Now he needs to work out how he can turn dull material into something exciting and fun.

Found-object art

Art can be a very interesting way of learning about yourself and your career choices. Art taps into your subconscious (those things that you don't know because they are inside of you) and brings them out. When we see the Mona Lisa (the painting of a woman smiling slightly) we wonder why she is not totally happy, we wonder what happened in her life or even what will happen to her next. Looking at that picture may also make us think about where we are not totally happy in our lives and what we can do about that situation.

If you want a different view of an issue or you want to remind yourself of your goals in a new way you can use an art project to help you.

For example, you could make a collage. A collage is a collection of different pieces of paper—bills, tickets, reports, words, and pictures—which you arrange and stick to or mount on a board. You might collect a series of pictures, which represent what your future work life looks like—an office overlooking the sea, a team of fun people, and a fancy car to show that you want a well-paying job. Your collage would be a piece of art that you could hang. You could look at it every day to remind yourself of your goals. Or you could look at it when you were feeling low and wanted inspiration about the future.

John could make something from these things that he found.

For example, a CD of music he loves from his childhood he found at a garage sale, a clip from YouTube which shows an eagle soaring up above an inspiring mountain range, a page from a law text book he found in the garbage at work, a cartoon character doll of Goofy he found in toy store, half a dollar bill he picked up in the street. The CD represents his past, when he was free to enjoy life and did not need to think about his career. He would listen to music with his friends and be totally happy. The clip from YouTube represents his future where he is free to soar in his career and inspire others. The law book is the tedious part of his work he hates right now. The cartoon character is him in the future: fun-loving, funny, and not caring what other people think! The half a dollar bill signifies his lack of value of himself. He could put these all together in a mixed media sculpture with the audio and video playing and not only would it be cool, but it would also be a symbol of his old and new life. Every time he saw it he would see something to motivate him to take the next step.

Something completely different

In this technique you get to choose what you do as a way of making sure that you keep focused on your vision and goals. As outsiders we often don't like to be pigeonholed. We want to have the freedom to choose. So this is the most unstructured choice. Let's see an example.

John might decide to write a song that sums up his hopes and fears.

Throughout the course of an hour, or a day, or weeks, he works on that song and each time he sings it, his heart hears more deeply his hopes, and those strengthen his resolve and sense of purpose. And each time he sings it, his fears are carried off into the breezes and his burdens are lightened.

Here the choice is yours. It could be a song, a poem, a play, or a movie. It could be teaching a class, making a presentation, or writing an article. Or it could be meditating every day on a key word that symbolizes your career journey. Or it could be going on a journey such that in every town you stopped you took a photograph, which related to you being a successful outsider. It's your project!

It is up to you choose a vehicle, a technique, a creative expression that helps you to focus on how you are going to take the next step on your journey toward greater outsider success in your career.

You've been introduced to several different processes for integrating what you have learned and then building on it to take into your future. I suggest you pick one process, just one, and commit to it, own it, make it a habit and stick with it so the insight and wisdom you've gained here will be reinforced and multiplied in the years ahead. Whatever you decide to do, your life will never be the same, as you make more conscious, deliberate, and better-informed choices.

THE CONSUMMATE SUCCESSFUL OUTSIDER: THE AUTHOR'S CONCLUDING REMARKS

I want to thank you for your courage in reading this book, and by so doing participating in its many challenging reviews and evaluation of important areas of your life. These areas include how we relate to others in the workplace, how they relate to us, and what we can do differently and better. They are not explored by the timid.

For me, an outsider as far back as I can remember, this has been a deeply personal journey, and if you get no other message, take to heart that you are not alone as an outsider. Your success as an outsider will not be defined by conquering all the problems and obstacles in your job, workplace, or career. They will always be there, and when they are solved, there will be new ones—such is the nature of the human condition that we enjoy the challenges, the strength they offer us, and the growth we gain.

You have the benefit of the many hard-fought lessons of the outsiders, great or unsung, that have blazed the trail before you. Only a few we have discussed in this book; many more are easily available to you when you are having a bad day or a bad year, and need a lift or inspiration.

Remember, jobs without problems don't pay much. Enjoy the challenges, celebrate the many wins and victories, however small—or especially the small ones, for they are stuff of good days and building blocks of good lives.

Good luck and stay true to yourself!
David Couper

ACKNOWLEDGMENTS

Firstly, I want to thank Ed and Teddy who are the most important people in my life and my sister Hazel and her family who have always been there for me even although they live many thousands of miles. I would have loved for my parents to have been here for this book but even though they are not with us I know that they are watching over its launch.

Secondly, I owe a huge thanks to everyone at Career-Press for making the publishing of this book so stress free! I also must thank John Willig and Randy Peyser who helped make this book possible. My editor John Shaw is a gift who helped me so much in making the manuscript what it is today and Loetta Earnest and Mary Pat Nally have been so supportive in making sure that everything gets done impeccably.

Finally, I am so happy that I found the University of Santa Monica. Completing my education there was a joy. Without my teachers, Mary and Ron Hulnick and Pat Peake, and my project team: Nancy, Maria, Patty and Manuel, I would have never completed this book. Thank you.

INDEX

ABOUT THE AUTHOR

David Couper is the author of seven books and is an award-winning career trainer and coach in the United States, Europe, and Asia. He has helped miserable outsiders become happy and successful at Fortune 100 companies, fast-food joints, and faith-based organizations. Couper has a BA in Communication, completed postgraduate work in education, and graduated with a Masters in Spiritual Psychology. He has been quoted in more than 30 different online and print publications. He lives in Los Angeles, California. For further information visit *www.davidcoupercoach.com*.